A Mismatch
of Salience

Explorations of the
nature of autism from
theory to practice

By Dr. Damian E M Milton

Pavilion

A Mismatch of Salience

Explorations of the nature of autism from theory to practice

By Dr. Damian EM Milton

© Pavilion Publishing and Media Ltd

The author has asserted his rights in accordance with the Copyright, Designs and Patents Act (1988) to be identified as the author of this work.

Published by:
Pavilion Publishing and Media Ltd
Blue Sky Offices, Cecil Pashley Way
Shoreham by Sea, West Sussex, BN43 5FF
Tel: 01273 434 943
Email: info@pavpub.com

Published 2017

ISBN: 978-1-911028-76-5

A catalogue record for this book is available from the British Library.

Author: Dr. Damian E M Milton
Editor: Mike Benge, Pavilion Publishing and Media Ltd
Cover design: Emma Dawe, Pavilion Publishing and Media Ltd
Layout design: Emma Dawe, Pavilion Publishing and Media Ltd
Printing: Print on Demand Worldwide

In association with the Participatory Autism Research Collective (PARC)

Contents

'Some things you miss because they're so tiny you overlook them. But some things you don't see because they're so huge. We were both looking at the same thing, seeing the same thing, talking about the same thing, thinking about the same thing, except he was looking, seeing, talking and *thinking*, from a completely different *dimension*.'

Robert M Pirsig, *Zen and the Art of Motorcycle Maintenance*

Foreword

Damian Milton has a tremendous facility in presenting his insider views on being autistic and challenging the received wisdom expounded by many neurotypical people. This collection of writings demonstrates this ability. His double empathy argument, discussed in the first chapter, 'So what exactly is autism?' suggests that it is not simply a matter of autistic people not understanding the communication and emotions of others, but that in turn, neurotypical people fail to understand the communication and language of autistic individuals. This is a powerful reframing of views on who has the difficulty. As Milton writes, viewing the 'autistic person' as the 'disordered other', can reduce an individual's sense of self-worth and self-esteem. His preference is to talk about embodied diversity rather than impairment to capture the many ways of being human. Other chapters cite the work of Laing, Szasz and others, and speak of the interaction of factors which contribute or lead to disability and mental illness, pointing out that both are context specific and that adjusting society and people's perspectives and responses to individuals promotes physical and mental well-being.

In later chapters, Damian turns to the production of knowledge in autism studies, showing that until recently, this knowledge was created almost entirely by non-autistic people on the outside looking in. Such endeavour is clearly and obviously flawed, both ethically and in terms of its insular perspective, yet continued for several decades. In all his work and writings, Damian has pushed for academics and researchers to involve autistic people in the design of research and its key questions at the outset, rather than merely being asked to comment on drafts of questions and instruments, or to review the final research report. He has succeeded in achieving such involvement for himself and has attained key positions in the National Autistic Society and within a number of universities in the UK. He has also significantly influenced others to consult children and young people and adults on the autism spectrum, His message is not confined to research but also to the design and implementation of services and interventions. The chapter 'So what exactly are autism interventions intervening with?' makes the point that autistic individuals are rarely asked for their views on what they think of the plans for them or for their views on interventions before these are implemented. Damian's work and energy have changed this practice in some spheres, but there is still a long way to go.

The chapters in this book will be read by many and so will have a wide reach and will prompt readers to consider their own position on how they view autism and the extent to which they truly involve and consult autistic individuals. This book has the potential to change and enhance what is provided and to alter how and when autistic children and adults across the autism spectrum are involved and engaged in research, the creation of knowledge, and in discussions about what might help and make a positive difference to their lives.

Dr Glenys Jones
University of Birmingham
August 2017

About the author

Damian works part-time for the National Autistic Society (NAS) as Head of Autism Knowledge and Expertise (Adults and Community) and sits on the scientific and advisory committee for Research Autism. Damian also teaches on the MA Education (Autism) programme at London South Bank University and has been a consultant for the Transform Autism Education (TAE) project and a number of projects for the Autism Education Trust (AET). In the summer of 2017, Damian joined the Tizard Centre, University of Kent, as a part-time lecturer to coincide with his work for the NAS. Damian's primary focus is on increasing the meaningful participation of autistic people and people with learning disabilities in the research process, and chairs the Participatory Autism Research Collective (PARC): www.PARCautism.co.uk.

Damian's interest in autism began when his son was diagnosed as autistic in 2005 at the age of two. Damian was also diagnosed with Asperger's in 2009 at the age of thirty-six.

Other books by Damian Milton and colleagues:
Milton D and Martin N (2017) *Autism and Intellectual Disability in Adults, Vol 2* (Eds). Hove: Pavilion Publishing.
Milton D and Martin N (2016) *Autism and Intellectual Disability in Adults, Vo. 1* (Eds). Hove: Pavilion Publishing.
Milton D, Mills R and Jones S (2016) *Ten rules for ensuring people with learning disabilities and those on the autism spectrum develop 'challenging behaviour'…and maybe what to do about it*. Hove: Pavilion Publishing.

'As a sociologist, autism researcher, academic, writer and advocate, Damian Milton has an extensive and informed grasp of the scientific and ethical principles that are key to any meaningful critique of current practice in autism. As a parent of a young autistic person and having received a diagnosis of Asperger syndrome himself in his 30s, Dr Milton is particularly well placed to comment on developments in

the field. His insights are invariably to the point and illuminating and will be invaluable to the wide community with a personal or professional interest in autism.' Prof Richard Mills

'Damian Milton is one of the most original thinkers in autism research today. These collected essays present a progressive and thoughtful perspective on autism which would be of value to scholars from both the sciences and the humanities.' Dr Sue Fletcher-Watson

'Damian's angle on issues in autism, from a sociological and philosophical perspective, has had a real impact in shifting perceptions. I hope this book will be widely read.'
Dr Dinah Murray

'A stunning collection of essays illuminating with brilliant insight the complex interface between autism and how it is understood by society. A must-read for all.' Dr Brett Heasman

'Damian Milton applies sociological and methodological rigour to key issues in the field of autism studies, including labelling and its impact, the impact of unexamined assumption on autism research, embodied experiences of autism, and human (neuro)diversity. His work is informative, thought-provoking and highly recommended.'
Dr Mitzi Waltz

'Dr Damian Milton is the brains and the inspiration behind The Participatory Autism Research Collective (PARC). Because of his energy, expertise and insider perspective, PARC has grown – without funding – to an international collective of autistic scholars working together to inform autism research authentically.' Prof Nicola Martin

A Mismatch of Salience: Explorations of the nature of autism from theory to practice
© Pavilion Publishing and Media Ltd and its licensors 2017.

Part one:
This thing called autism

The term 'autism' and how to apply it is certainly not without its controversies. Ever since its origins as a clinical term there have been theoretical debates regarding the 'essential nature' of what it is that the term is referring to, or even if it is referring to a definable 'condition'. The first chapter in this collection addresses the issue of what exactly autism is. This chapter was produced as a resource for lead educational practitioners and linked to the Autism Education Trust's National Standards for Schools. This chapter is followed by a reflection of the social issues that can impact on the mental well-being of autistic people and a deconstruction of 'pathological demand avoidance'. The final chapter in this section is a reflection on the notion of 'impairment' in relation to the diversity of embodied experiences one can find among the autistic population.

So what exactly is autism?

A version of this essay was first published as a resource for the Autism Education Trust Practitioner Competency Framework (Wittemeyer *et al*, 2012).

Introduction

Autism was once considered to be an extremely rare 'disorder' that affected a tiny proportion of the population, however in recent decades the numbers of those diagnosed as being somewhere on the wider 'autism spectrum' has massively increased to an approximated figure of 1 in 100. Autism has been variously described as everything from an evil spirit that robs parents of their children, to a fundamental asset of human evolution as a person with a differing style of thinking. It is no wonder that the 'enigma' still evades simplistic description, as scientists and psychologists search in vain for the cause of 'what it is'. This article attempts to help the reader navigate through the maze of explanations that have been suggested and some of the problems such explanatory models possess. Such a text can never be fully comprehensive however, and so the reader is encouraged never to think that they understand what 'autism is', but to strive to understand the 'autistic people' they work with as well as they can, and to see this as an ongoing process and mutually respectful interaction. The term 'autism' was first used by a psychiatrist called Bleuler in 1911 to try and describe a type of what was then called 'schizophrenia'. His descriptions, however, only show a passing resemblance to how autism is thought of today:

> *'The schizophrenics who have no more contact with the outside world live in a world of their own. They have encased themselves with their desires and wishes ... they have cut themselves off as much as possible from any contact with the external world. This detachment from reality with the relative and absolute predominance of the inner life, we term autism.'* (Bleuler, 1911, cited in Parnas *et al*, 2002: 131).

In the 1940s, two psychiatrists working separately, one called Kanner, the other Asperger, were studying small groups of children deemed as having some form of 'childhood schizophrenia'. Both found that with the groups of children they were working with a set of distinct symptoms were being identified that were markedly different from schizophrenia as it was conceived of at the time. Kanner's work laid the foundation for early accounts of autism, while the work of Asperger was left largely undiscovered until the 1970s. Definitions of what autism is, and also what caused an autistic developmental pattern in children have been hotly contested ever since, including an unfortunate era where autism was thought to be a reaction to 'refrigerator mothers', a theory long since shown to be totally untrue.

A note on terminology

There is much current debate regarding the terminology related to autism. This article will resist 'people first' phrasing, in accordance with other 'autistic voices' (Sinclair, 1993; Sainsbury, 2000):

> *'We are not people who 'just happen to have autism'; it is not an appendage that can be separated from who we are as people, nor is it something shameful that has to be reduced to a sub-clause.'*
> (Sainsbury, 2000: 12)

The descriptors of 'autistic person/people' and 'autistic spectrum' will be used, and the use of the terms Autistic Spectrum Disorder/Condition (ASD/ASC) are avoided due to the 'medical model' connotations (see section on models of disability on pxx) associated with these phrases and the offense that they may cause.

Diagnosis and the triad of impairments

One of the most important developments in the history of autism in Britain was the work of Wing and Gould (1979) and the subsequent widening of the 'autism spectrum' to include 'Asperger syndrome'. This work largely created the contemporary definition of autism as a 'triad of impairments' in social communication, social interaction, and imagination (repetitive interests/activities). Since this time, diagnostic systems have changed to reflect these changes in definition.

The most commonly used definition of autism that one sees today is that it is a:

'...lifelong developmental disability that affects how a person communicates with, and relates to, other people. It also affects how they make sense of the world around them.' (NAS, 2012a)

Although this definition of autism is much contested (see section on the double empathy problem), such a definition of behavioural deficit and impairment has come to characterise both the DSM-IV (1994)[1] and ICD-10 (1992) diagnostic criteria. Autism is thus diagnosed according to 'qualitative' impairments in all three areas: social interaction, communication, and rigidity of thinking.

Cognition – an impaired theory of mind?

One of the most enduring psychological theories concerning autism has been the assertion that the key universal core 'deficit' found in autistic spectrum conditions is an impaired 'theory of mind' (Baron-Cohen *et al*, 1985). 'Theory of Mind' refers to the ability to empathise with others and imagine their thoughts and feelings, in order to comprehend and predict the behaviour of others (also called 'mind-reading' and 'mentalising'). Baron-Cohen *et al* (1985) found that 80% of autistic children between the ages of 6-16 failed at false belief tasks. These findings were also repeated in subsequent studies using people rather than dolls, such as in the 'Sally-Ann' test (Leslie & Frith, 1988).

This theory has been criticised on a number of levels however: task failure on false-belief tasks could be due to difficulties in language processing or memory (Eisenmajer & Prior, 1991), or a lack of motivation to deceive (DeGelder, 1987). Some theorists questioned its applicability to all on the spectrum when 20% of children passed such tests, or its value for explaining all the aspects of what constituted the autistic difference (Happe, 1994a). 'Theory of mind' deficit as a general theory has been subsequently revised in order to differentiate between an ability to ascertain the feelings of others, and the development of 'affective' empathy once those feelings are recognised. Later studies by Baron-Cohen (1992) and Happe (1994b) also found that the ability to successfully complete theory of mind tasks increased with age and IQ, suggesting a delayed 'mentalising' capacity. It has also been argued that a deficit in 'social functioning' cannot be solely located within an individual, and that what is being seen as a 'theory of mind' deficit is more to do with a breakdown in communication between two people who process information very differently.

In this sense, there exists a 'double empathy problem' in that both autistic and neurotypical people have a severe difficulty in understanding each other, as neither share the same frame of reference within social

---

1   Now DSM-V (2013).

interactions (Milton, 2012a). This is most evident by how empathetic autistic people seem to be with the similarities they share with one another, an opportunity that has vastly improved with the use of internet technology.

Executive functioning

Executive function refers to the ability to maintain an appropriate problem-solving strategy in order to attain a future goal. Evidence from first-hand accounts suggest that autistic people have 'difficulties' with switching attention, and adverse reactions to interference with attention (Tammet, 2006). However, there is also evidence that individuals diagnosed with Asperger syndrome have performed well on executive functioning tests such as the 'Tower of London' test, and that other clinical groups can struggle with such tests, suggesting a lack of specificity to people diagnosed autistic.

Dawson *et al* (2007) found that autistic people can often do very well at non-verbal IQ tests and problem-solving tasks that do not require verbal processing. This would suggest that executive planning for non-verbal tasks is separable in brain functioning from verbal tasks, or that this weakness in verbal response tests is not due to an executive functioning deficit. It could be suggested that, rather than such evidence suggesting an overarching deficit in executive processing, there is a difference that exists within the way autistic executive processing operates. Yet rather than an impairment or deficiency, this is better articulated by the theory of monotropism (see section on monotropism).

A weak drive toward central coherence

In her review of psychological theories regarding autism, Happe (1994a) suggested that one of the major difficulties with the theories of 'theory of mind deficit' (see section on theory of mind) and 'executive functioning deficit' (see section on executive functioning) was their lack of explanatory value when considering autistic 'strengths' and 'talents'. For example, Shah and Frith (1983) found that autistic people outperformed non-autistic people at 'embedded figure tests', and picking out details from a visual array. These tasks required the ignoring of 'overall meaning' in order to be solved, and was followed by similar findings using a 'block design' task (Shah & Frith, 1993).

The Gestalt psychologist Koffka (1935) suggested that great effort is needed for people to resist a tendency to see a forcefully-created 'gestalt' or whole picture, in order to see constituent parts of that whole. Happe (1994a) suggested that autistic people had a 'weak drive for central coherence', and so have problems accounting for overall contextual meanings, while simultaneously having advantages in processing details or parts of an overall context.

Mottron *et al* (1999), as well as Baron-Cohen (2008) point out a difficulty for this theory to contend with, that being how autistic people are able to process the 'whole picture'. For instance, in the Navon test (a letter made up of smaller letters of a differing character – e.g. an A made up of Hs), autistic people are able to process the larger letter, yet have a tendency to be drawn to the smaller.

Empathising-Systemising (E-S) Theory

In part a response to the criticisms made of the 'theory of mind' hypothesis that it did not take into account the non-social differences involved in autism, Baron-Cohen (2008) argued that, along with 'delays and deficits' in empathy, the strengths found among autistic people could be explained by an intact or even superior skill in 'systemising'. This area of strength refers to the drive to analyse and construct systems, defined by rules that govern them, in order to predict how systems will behave. Baron-Cohen (2008) distinguishes a number of systems from collectible systems (for example distinguishing between a set of inanimate objects like stones) to abstract (such as musical notation), and social systems (such as management hierarchy). Rules are obtained by noting if two phenomena are associated in a systematic or causal way.

Baron-Cohen (2008) explains the commonly associated feature of autism of a 'lack of an ability to generalise' between situations, as symptomatic of a systemising mentality, as a 'strong systemiser' sees each system as unique, where differences between systems are of greater interest than their commonalities.

> '*A good systemiser is a splitter, not a lumper, since lumping things together can lead to missing key differences that enable you to predict how these two things behave differently. Seen in this light, it is the neurotypical person who has a difficulty, skating over differences that might be very important.*' (Baron-Cohen, 2008: 70-71)

This ability to systemise can be a seen as a defence against inaccurate conclusions being drawn through an under-analysis and premature generalising of any given phenomenon. The E-S theory of autism has also been extended to the 'extreme male brain' theory of autism (Baron-Cohen, 2008). This theory was derived initially from how women show a preference for empathising and men systemising. From this standpoint, the autistic 'cognitive style' can be seen as an extreme example of a typical male outlook (a view first postulated by Asperger, 1944, cited in Baron-Cohen, 2008). Baron-Cohen (2008) supports this theory through the use of quotient personality profiles, yet also the development of different skills at different points of development between typically developing boys and girls, and furthermore, that men on average are quicker in the embedded-figures test.

Baron-Cohen's (2008) use of quotient questionnaires to measure personality are very reminiscent of psychometric personality testing, a tradition highly influenced by personality trait theory, exemplified in the work of Eysenck and Rachman (1965). Trait theory rests upon the assumption that a consistent structure of personality resides in each individual person, yet perceptions of attributes related to others may have more to do with those doing the perceiving than those being perceived. Traits from this view are nothing more than constructions in the 'eye of the beholder' that reflect a world view of the perceiver, rooted within cultural ideologies and not a reflection of inner psychological dispositions of those being rated. Mischel (1968, cited in Butt, 2007) also criticised the questionnaires used in psychometric testing, with words such as 'often' being construed to mean different things to different people and are thus an invalid indicator of some 'underlying trait', accordingly, behaviour is theorised as much more context specific and socially situated.

Richards (2002) suggests that traits may be no more than an artefact of the measurement system used to analyse them. Richards (2002) also criticises the circularity of trait theories and questions whether 'attitudes' even exist as 'natural' phenomena. It can be argued that the approach adopted by trait theory offers little more than a description of behaviour and displays a circularity of reasoning, for example: explaining aggressive behaviour by saying someone is aggressive.

Monotropism – a different cognitive style?

The theory of Monotropism (Murray *et al*, 2005) argues that the central core feature in autism refers to an atypical strategy being employed in the distribution of attention, which is suggested to be the basis of the 'restricted range of interests' criteria inherent in the diagnostic criteria of both the DSM-IV (1994)[2] and ICD-10 (1992), and further found in the testimonies of subjective experience from autistic people themselves (Grandin, 1995; Lawson, 1998; Williams, 1994).

---

2   Now DSM-V (2013).

Monotropism suggests that the amount of attention available to an individual at any one time is necessarily limited, as can be found among numerous cognitive studies. Thus the shaping of many cognitive processes depends upon a competition between mental processes for this scarce resource. Murray *et al* (2005) propose that strategies for the way attention is used is normally distributed, and to a large degree genetically determined, between those with a broad use of attention, and those who concentrate attention on a small number of 'interests' (likened to the difference between a dissipated 'diffused light' and a 'torch beam'). The authors propose that those at the tightly focused end of this spectrum are those diagnosed as on the autism spectrum.

It is suggested by Murray *et al* (2005) that social interaction, the use of language, and the shifting of object attention (implicated by other psychological theories) are all tasks that require a broad attention, and are inhibited by a narrow use of attention.

This theory suggests a number of features found in autistic subjective accounts that are not attended to by the other psychological theories, including E-S theory (see section on E-S theory). For instance, how individuals on the autism spectrum show a tendency toward either being passionately interested in a task or phenomena, or not interested at all, or how an unanticipated change 'within the attentional tunnel' can lead to a catastrophic disconnection from a previously 'safe' state of mind.

If employing a monotropic interest system, the ability to use information gained in the past is compromised, as information is gained only in relation to a narrow set of interests. Thus 'topdown' or 'whole picture' processing is not 'dispreferred' as such, but will tend to be idiosyncratic and resistant to change or criticism. This resistance is not fully explained by a 'systemising' tendency (Baron-Cohen, 2008).

Monotropism also suggests a reason for the sensory integration difficulties found in the accounts of autistic people, as they suggest there is a 'hyper-awareness' of phenomena within the attentional tunnel, but hypo-sensitivity to phenomena outside of it. Also, that an interest in the social world may not occur in the early years of life:

> *'We suggest that the uneven skills profile in autism depends on which interests have been fired into monotropic superdrive and which have been left unstimulated by any felt experience.'*
> (Murray *et al* 2005: 143).

Indeed, the recognition of others may only occur if connected to the fulfilling of interests that the autistic individual has, otherwise the existence of others may not be registered at all. A monotropic focus leads to a fragmented view of the world, and from such a viewpoint it is exceptionally hard to make sense of social interactions, leading potentially to both apparent and real 'theory of mind' difficulties. Rather than being a 'core deficit' however, this is described as a tendency produced as a consequence of a monotropic interest system.

Autism from the 'inside-out'

Psychological models of autism tend to work on the cognitive level of explanation, with some attempting to make links to biological and neurological data. In order to produce cognitive models, all of them rely on accounts of behaviour to make inferences from. A major criticism of these models is that they are formed (with the exception of monotropism theory) from a perspective of a cognitive psychology overly restricted by its total adherence to scientific method as the gold standard, which do not value the input of 'autistic voices', or that of sociological viewpoints on autism. This has come about for a number of reasons, one of which being the splitting of levels of explanation into subject 'silos' (Arnold, 2010). Another was the triumphant victory that biomedical explanations earned at the expense of Bettleheim's (1967) theory of the 'refrigerator mother'. This victory would not just produce a rejection of this theory however, but it seems a total rejection of psycho-sociological reflection upon what it is to be autistic, a fatal flaw that only alienated the voices of autistic people further. The victory spared the mother, yet lay the blame at the neurology of the 'autistic person' themselves, in the sense that there was something medically deficient about the 'autistic person', and if one could only find the site of the 'lesion' one could find a 'cure' (Happe, 1994a). Assumptions of what autism is are enshrined in the diagnostic criteria of the DSM-IV[3] (1994) and ICD-10 (1992) and based upon interpretations of observed behavioural traits. All the psychological theories base their models within this criterion of behaviour-led framework, although in the monotropism theory, this is thankfully balanced by the accounts of lived experience of 'autistic people' themselves, including one of the authors of the paper, Wendy Lawson.

The current psychological models seem somewhat inadequate at drawing the links between biology and behaviour, but even more so between biology and the lived experience of autistic subjectivity, often attempting to obscure the 'autistic voice' or ignore it, in an attempt to reduce autistic behaviours to definable objective criteria. The theory of monotropism, is a welcome departure from this theoretical dominance however, largely basing its account in subjective accounts. In so doing, this theory is more applicable

---

3   Now DSM-V (2013).

to the vast array of subjective differences experienced by autistic people, although perhaps not all. Unfortunately, it does not seem to have achieved the widespread recognition enjoyed by the other theories.

> '...right from the start, from the time someone came up with the word 'autism', the condition has been judged from the outside, by its appearances, and not from the inside according to how it is experienced.' (Williams, 1996: 14)

The spiky profile, stress and sensory overload

One of the key aspects of the experience of being autistic is that of having a 'spiky' or 'uneven' set of abilities and capacities. It is the feeling of many on the spectrum, however, that this spiky profile is often unrecognised by service providers and support workers. Verbal 'autistic people' are often incorrectly assumed to be capable in areas in which they struggle, while those with less verbal skills are often incorrectly assumed to be lacking in skills, 'strengths', ability or potential for example. One of the most important aspects of autism that for many years went fairly unrecognised was that of sensory sensitivities. Autistic people often report both hyper-sensitivities to sounds, lights, smells and touch, but also 'hypo' sensitivities, where such sensations fail to register. Like most things about the autism spectrum, such sensitivities will vary from person to person and across contexts, and can be quite unpredictable from the viewpoint of someone not on the autism spectrum to observe and understand. A common pattern found (but not universally) is that of hyper-sensitivities to sensations of external events, and hypo-sensitivities with internal feelings, such as a sense of balance, or knowing where one's own body 'begins and ends' (perhaps due to a 'monotropic' sensory focus when acting upon the environment – see section on monotropism). With a fragmented information processing style, sensory integration can become a challenge for 'autistic people', thus a 'low-arousal' approach in educational environments is often needed.

There is a growing body of evidence that has begun to link autism with irregular levels of the hormone cortisol, which affects 'arousal' and levels of stress. The experience of stress is one that is nigh-on universal among autistic people, along with the sense of overload (whether sensory or emotional). Such irregularities could lead to a person becoming overly lethargic and/or overly stimulated at different times throughout the course of a day. This can produce difficulties in everything from wrongly attributed 'laziness', to challenges getting to sleep at night. The reactions of autistic 'meltdown' and 'shutdown' can be viewed as extreme expressions of the 'fight or flight' response. To an outsider perspective, one may see no immediate stressor and trigger to such events, yet this is generally less the case when viewed from someone who is autistic themselves. Thus, working closely with the autistic person in their care, is essential for practitioners to learn how that individual operates within a variety of contexts, what external events are likely to cause distress, and take a general 'low-arousal' approach to managing the learning environment. When in a state of meltdown or shutdown, the best option where possible, is to leave the autistic person alone, to reduce all external stressors, and then when they are able to calm themselves, attempt to engage with something predictable and comforting to the 'autistic person'. Ethically speaking, behavioural outcomes should never be prioritised over reflection regarding the processes that one uses to accomplish such tasks and the stress that such processes can create for the autistic person.

> '[Behavioural strategies]...may feel like a senseless ritual of abuse, regardless of its 'good' intentions.' (Williams, 1996: 51)

Episodic and factual memory

The fragmentation of experience often cited by autistic people can cause difficulties with regards to constructing an autobiographical narrative of self (Millward *et al*, 2000). Both Millward *et al* (2000) and Crane and Goddard (2008) suggest that a 'deficit' can be found in the personal 'episodic memories' of people on the autism spectrum, yet not with regard to semantic factual memory. It is argued here, however, that factual information can also become fragmented in the consciousness of autistic people and that this is again dependent on the particular 'spiky profile' of an individual and the context one is situated within. Potential challenges regarding episodic memory were also found in the research of Goddard *et al* (2007), where longer periods of time were needed for autistic people to retrieve personal memories, and with fewer specific episodes remembered. Goldman (2008) found that there was a reduced number of emotional 'high points' to be found in the personal narratives of autistic people (although this must also be read in context of the social lives that autistic people lead). Milton (2012b) suggests that the use of photography as memory aides can be of great use to autistic people with regard to 'putting the self back into the picture', not just in the sense of visual timetables, but in a host of other techniques, including: photo-montage, collage, scrap books, photo sorting, and where possible, building and reconstructing narratives regarding particular photographs or sets of them. It should also be remembered though that not all autistic people are visual learners, and some need more direct and tangible symbols of meaning in order to navigate an environment, and to begin to build a sense of self over time. In these instances, methods such as 'objects of reference' would be recommended (Community Matters, 2012).

Intersubjectivity – the 'double empathy problem'

The models of autism as presented by cognitive psychological theories, much like the triad of impairments, locate the difficulties faced by autistic people solely within the brains/minds of the 'autistic person', rather than the world in which they inhabit, or in the relations and interactions people have, that can lead to a sense of total disconnection through to a mutual shared sense of 'social reality'. A number of sociologists view 'versions of perceptual truth' as contested and negotiated in interaction. Milton (2011; 2012a) argues that the social subtext of a situation is never a given, but actively constructed in the interactions people have with one another. From this point of view, it is illogical to talk of an individual having a 'social' deficit of some sort.

Rather, that in the case of when autistic people and those not on the autism spectrum attempt to interact, it is both that have a problem in terms of empathising with each other: a 'double empathy problem'. Indeed, autistic writers have been talking of empathy being a 'two-way street' for many years (e.g. Sinclair, 1993). A more serious problem ensues however, when one side of an interaction are able to impose their own views of a situation onto the other. This can also lead to the subsequent internalisation of this dominant outsider view and a loss of connection with one's sense of authentic selfhood.

'I had virtually no socially-shared nor consciously, intentionally expressed, personhood beyond this performance of a non-autistic 'normality' with which I had neither comprehension, connection, nor identification. This disconnected constructed facade was accepted by the world around me when my true and connected self was not. Each spoonful of its acceptance was a shovel full of dirt on the coffin in which my real self was being buried alive...' (Williams, 1996: 243)

The medical and social models of disability

Within wider disability politics and advocacy, as well as the sociological study of disability, there are a number of 'models' that have been implemented. The two most frequently mentioned are those of the 'medical' and 'social' model of health, illness and disability. The traditional medical model would view disability as a functional deficit that belonged to the disabled person.

This view of disability was widely challenged however by disability activists and sociologists that suggested that it was society that created barriers to the participation of disabled people in social life. For instance, the problem of access to a building for a wheelchair user being the steps needed to enter it. The social model of disability suggests that society disables people by the way structures are designed. Many theorists go further, and suggest that people are further psychologically 'disabled' by a culture and ideology of 'normalcy' (Goodley, 2011; Reeve, 2011; Milton, 2012c).

The widespread recognition of a social model approach to making adjustments to increase inclusive practices has been greater for those with 'visible disabilities' than those that are more 'hidden'. An important aspect of the social model would suggest that it is the disabled person who is the 'expert' on their own requirements. In the case of autism, however, it is not always possible for the autistic person to achieve communicating their intents to those who provide care for them. This has as much to do with the service provider as it does the autistic person though (see section on the double empathy problem).

A model widely used in health and social care theory is that of the 'bio-psycho-social' model of health (Engel, 1977). This model suggests that when looking at the needs of a 'client', one needs to approach a 'medical' issue in terms of the biological, psychological, and social state/situation that the person is in. This is a vague model at present though, with little agreement between academic theorists to the weighting of these areas, or how they interrelate to produce disability. In terms of the education of autistic people, the tradition has been to highlight the biological and psychological aspects of the 'syndrome', but it is argued here that this has been a mistake.

A case in point: mental well-being

Much literature on autism would suggest that autistic people are in some way predisposed to difficulties in psychiatric ill-health, including anxiety, depression, and catatonia (NAS, 2012b). This view however is a 'medical model' view of mental well-being (see section on models of disability) that does not account for the 'problems of living' people on the autism spectrum have in navigating a social world that was not designed for their needs (to apply a more social model to the situation). The lack of opportunities 'autistic people' have in society, coupled with the social stigma of being seen as having a pathologically deviant cognition, is added to further by the trauma of 'passing as normal' (Lawson, 2008).

In 2010, a group of young people on the autism spectrum made a film for the NAS regarding mental ill-health and relevant service provision entitled 'Open Your Mind' (NAS, 2010). It is recommended here that such initiatives are seen as the start of further exploration into how best to support autistic people who experience mental ill-health.

The language of autism – not just semantics

For many philosophers, the way we talk about something is 'more than just words', but frames the way we think about ourselves and one another. By viewing the 'autistic person' as the 'disordered other', it can reduce an individual's sense of self-worth and self-esteem. Dekker (2011) suggested that autistic advocates used a language that carried more positive connotations when talking about the autistic difference.

Implications for practice – from modification to mutuality

There is a spectrum in theory and practice more generally regarding service provision for autistic people. At one end sit those adhering to techniques of behavioural modification, so that children are socialised into what are deemed appropriate behaviours of socially functional future roles. At the other extreme of this spectrum is an ethos of interactive mutuality concerned with the empowerment of individuals and communities, and where dominance and imposition of authority is seen as 'dysfunctional'. Expressions of these extremes could be said to be found more frequently in discourses regarding best educational practice for autistic people, ranging from the efforts of the Lovaas model of Applied Behavioural Analysis, through to child-focused and democratic educational ideological preferences. These narratives and practices can be said to be embedded within the wider discursive debate that exists between the medical and social models of disability as played out in the field of autism. It is the view of this author that there is an increasing complacency around the idea that leads professionals and practitioners to have a good understanding of what 'good autism practice' entails, for me this is an ongoing imperfect process of interaction and should never be seen as a given.

> *'We have to challenge these myths and stereotypes about autism and work to advance an understanding that is based on better quality research, but also on the real life experiences of those of us on the autism spectrum rather than a conversation that talks about us, without us. By taking that step together, we will see more progress for self-advocates, providers and families.'* (Ne'eman, 2011)

Five key points for educational practitioners to remember

- Respect the individual learning style of the pupil – work with it, not against it.
- Always consider sensory issues.
- Always consider how your processing of information may be very different to that of the pupil in your care (utilise interests).
- Stress is a key issue – reduce input when people are over stressed.
- Collaborate for consistency in approach.

References

American Psychiatric Association (1994) *Diagnostic and Statistical Manual of Mental Disorders, 4th edition (DSM-IV)*. Washington: APA.

Arnold (2010) *The Medium is the Message*. London: University College London.

Baron-Cohen S (1992) Out of sight or out of mind? Another look at deception in autism. *Journal of Child Psychology and Psychiatry*. **33** (7) 1141–1155.

Baron-Cohen S (2008) *Autism and Asperger Syndrome: The facts*. Oxford: Oxford University Press.

Baron-Cohen S, Leslie A & Frith U (1985) Does the Autistic Child Have a 'Theory of Mind'? *Cognition* **21** 37–46.

Betttleheim B (1967) *The Empty Fortress: Infantile autism and the birth of the self*. New York: The Free Press.

Butt T (2007) Individual differences. In: D Langbridge and S. Taylor (eds) *Critical Readings in Social Psychology*. Milton Keynes: Open University.

Community Matters (2012) *Objects of Reference* [online]: Available at: www.communicationmatters.org.uk/page/objects-of-reference (accessed July 2017).

Crane L & Goddard L (2008) Episodic and semantic autobiographical memory in adults with autism spectrum disorders. *Journal of Autism and Developmental Disorders* **38** (3) 498–506.

Dawson M, Soulieres I, Gernsbacher M & Mottron L (2007) The level and nature of autistic intelligence. *Psychological Science* **18** (8) 657–662.

DeGelder B (1987) On not having a theory of mind. *Cognition* **27** 285–290.

Dekker M (2011) *Owning the Languages of Autism* [online]. Peterborough: Autscape.

Eisenmajer R & Prior M (1991) Cognitive linguistic correlates of 'theory of mind' ability in autistic children. *British Journal of Developmental Psychology* **9** 351–364.

Engel G (1977) The need for a new medical model: a challenge for biomedicine. *Science* **196** 129–136.

Eysenck H & Rachman S (1965/2007) Dimensions of Personality. In: D Langbridge and S Taylor (eds) *Critical Readings in Social Psychology*. Milton Keynes: Open University.

Goddard L, Howlin P, Dritschel B & Patel T (2007) Autobiographical memory and social problem-solving in asperger syndrome. *Journal of Autism and Developmental Disorders* **37** 291–300.

Goldman S (2008) Brief report: narratives of personal events in children with autism and developmental language disorders: unshared memories.', *Journal of Autism and Developmental Disorders* **38** 1982–1988.

Goodley (2011) *Disability Studies: An interdisciplinary introduction*. London: Sage.

Grandin T (1995) *Thinking in Pictures*. New York: Vintage.

Happe F (1994a) *Autism: an introduction to psychological theory*. London: UCL Press.

Happe F (1994b) Annotation: psychological theories of autism: the 'theory of mind' account and rival theories. *Journal of Child Psychology and Psychiatry* **35** 215–229.

Koffka K (1935) *Principles of Gestalt Psychology*. New York: Harcourt.

Lawson W (1998) *Life Behind Glass: A personal account of autism spectrum disorder*. London: Jessica Kingsley.

Lawson, W. (2008) *Concepts of Normality: The Autistic and Typical Spectrum*. London: Jessica Kingsley.

Leslie A & Frith U (1988) Autistic children's understanding of seeing, knowing and believing. *British Journal of Developmental Psychology* **6** 315–324.

Millward C, Powell S, Messer D & Jordan R (2000) Recall for self and other in autism: Children's memory for events experienced by themselves and their peers. *Journal of Autism and Developmental Disorders* **30** (1) 15–28.

Milton D (2011) Filling in the gaps, a micro-sociological analysis of autism. *Theorising Normalcy and the Mundane, 2nd International Conference*. Manchester Metropolitan University.

Milton D (2012a) On the Ontological Status of Autism: the 'Double Empathy Problem'. *Disability and Society* **27** (6) 883–887.

Milton D (2012b) Fragments: putting the self back into the picture. *Children, Youth, Family and Disability Conference*. Manchester Metropolitan University.

Milton D (2012c) Embodied Sociality and the Conditioned Relativism of Dispositional Diversity. *Theorising Normalcy and the Mundane, 3rd International Conference.* University of Chester.

Mottron L, Burack J, Stauder J & Robaey P (1999) Perceptual processing among highfunctioning persons with autism. *Journal of Child Psychology and Psychiatry.* **40** (2) 203–212.

Murray D, Lesser M & Lawson W (2005) Attention, monotropism and the diagnostic criteria for autism. *Autism* **9** (2) 136–156.

National Autistic Society (2010) *Open your mind* [online]. Available at: http://www.autism.org.uk/get-involved/campaign/england/young-campaigners-group/our-resources/film.aspx (accessed September 2017).

National Autistic Society (2012a) *What is Autism?* [online]. Available at: www.autism.org.uk/about-autism/autism-and-asperger-syndrome-an-introduction/what-is-autism.aspx, (accessed September 2017).

National Autistic Society (2012b) *Mental Health and Asperger Syndrone* [online]. Available at: www.autism.org.uk/working-with/health/mental-health-and-asperger-syndrome.aspx (accessed July 2011).

Ne'eman A (2011) *Question and answer interview* [online]. Available at: www.talkaboutautism.org.uk/community/live-qa-events/010611-ari-neeman (accessed June 2011).

Parnas J, Bovet P & Zahavi D (2002) Schizophrenic autism: clinical pathology and pathogenic implications. *World Psychiatry* **1** (3) 131–136.

Reeve D (2011) Ableism within disability studies: the myth of the reliable and contained body. *Theorising Normalcy and the Mundane, 2nd International Conference.* Manchester Metropolitan University.

Richards G (2002) *Putting Psychology in its Place: A critical historical overview (2nd ed.).* Hove: Routledge.

Sainsbury C (2000) *Martian in the Playground: Understanding the schoolchild with asperger's syndrome.* Bristol: Lucky Duck.

Shah A & Frith U (1983) An islet of ability in autistic children: a research note. *Journal of Child Psychology and Psychiatry* **24** 613–620.

Shah A & Frith U (1993) Why do autistic individuals show superior performance on the Block Design task? *Journal of Child Psychology and Psychiatry* **34** 1351–1364.

Sinclair J (1993) *Don't Mourn For Us* [online]: Available at: www.autreat.com/dont_mourn.html (accessed September 2017).

Tammet D (2006) *Born on a Blue Day.* London: Hodder and Stoughton.

Williams D (1994) *Somebody Somewhere.* London: Doubleday.

Williams D (1996) *Autism: An Inside-Out Approach.* London: Jessica Kingsley.

Wing L & Gould J (1979) Severe Impairments of Social Interaction and Associated Abnormalities in Children: Epidemiology and Classification. *Journal of Autism and Childhood Schizophrenia* **9** 11–29.

Wittemeyer K, English A, Jones G, Lyn-Cook L & Milton D (2012) *The Autism Education Trust Professional Competency Framework.* London: Autism Education Trust.

World Health Organisation (1992) *The International Classification of Mental and Behavioural Disorders: Clinical Descriptions and Diagnostic Guidelines, 10th edition (ICD-10)*. Geneva: WHO.

'Problems in living' and the mental well-being of autistic people

This essay was first published over two editions of Asperger United magazine (editions 71 and 72) in 2012.

Within the history of psychiatry and psychology, there are some who would argue that some kind of neurological defect will one day be found for all 'disorders' of thinking and behaviour, locating the 'problem' within a deficient and dysfunctional brain. There has also been, however, a movement for many decades that has suggested that mental illness was a 'myth', at least when it came to illnesses of the 'mind' which had no physical manifestation in some kind of damage to the brain. The former position would suggest that people cannot have psychological 'troubles' due to differences of social position. In the accounts of many writers and theorists from the 1960s onwards (like Thomas Szasz, RD Laing and Peter Breggin), biological causes were being wrongly attributed to 'problems in living'.

In his article 'The Myth of Mental Illness', written in 1960, Thomas Szasz argued that the perception of 'mental symptoms' entailed a comparison of the patient's conceptual beliefs with those of the observer and the dominant values of the society within which they live. He suggested that many of these so-called 'symptoms' were not due to some underlying damage to the brain, but were symptomatic of the stress inherent in social interaction. The definition of an illness, whether physical or mental, is often referred to as a deviation from a 'norm', yet for mental health 'deviations' these can only be judged, Szasz argued, psycho-socially and ethically, while the 'remedy' for such ills is one of psycho-pharmaceutical intervention. The only evidence that a 'mental illness' existing, being the psychiatrist being told or shown of a behaviourally defined symptom. Diagnosis for Szasz is thus a value judgement on whether or not behaviours are deemed within 'acceptable' limits and norms. In essence, people were being placed into scapegoated and stigmatised social categories.

Like Szasz, the work of RD Laing challenged the orthodoxy that mental illness was a biological phenomenon, with no connection to social context, or 'problems in living'. Laing suggested that psychiatry was built upon false assumptions, diagnosing illness by behavioural conduct, but treating by medical intervention. Laing however, also suggested that mental ill health could be a transformative episode, where the individual could gain important insights. A similar thought was expressed by the Polish psychologist Dabrowski in his work on 'gifted' children that were also 'over-sensitive'. In my own reading of Dabrowski, he was attempting to theorise about a kind of sub-group of autistic people that I myself could be said to belong to, characterised by a passive, hyper-sensitive disposition.

The idea that psychiatry was a genuine branch of medicine was also challenged by a number of notable theorists, such as Michel Foucault, Erving Goffman and David Rosenhan. More recently, similar arguments have been found in the work of Peter Breggin and in the controversial work of Sammi Timini who has suggested that the diagnosis of autism should be abolished. These theorists were often not opposed to the practice of psychiatry as such, as long as the therapeutic relationship was contractual, rather than coercive, between consenting adults, and without state intervention.

Many psychiatrists regard Szasz, Laing and others with similar views as pariahs of the profession, and would rather suggest that 'mental illnesses' are becoming ever more measurable and testable in a scientific fashion, and medications have been shown to be 'effective' in treating illnesses such as depression (although this is still hugely debatable). This 'medical model' of 'mental illness' has been dominant in discussions regarding autistic people having psychiatric 'co-morbidities', as evidenced in The NAS article 'Mental Health and Asperger Syndrome'. This article discusses a variety of ailments that could affect autistic people: depression, anxiety and catatonia. What this article often seems to do however, is to frame 'problems in living' in medical terminology, located the source of the 'problem' in the 'dysfunctional' autistic person, rather than in a 'dysfunctional society' within which they live:

> *'People with Asperger syndrome are particularly prone to anxiety disorders as a consequence of the social demands made upon them.'* (NAS, 2011)

The article then suggests that a good way to manage anxiety would be to use 'behavioural techniques', or relaxation therapies, or possibly drug treatments (including SSRI antidepressants). If anxiety is being caused by 'social demands' that are placed upon one, then perhaps these are not the most appropriate 'interventions'!

When reviewing 'psychological' treatments for 'mood disorders', the article states that the primary treatment is cognitive behavioural therapy:

'...as it is effective in changing the way a person thinks and responds to feelings such as anxiety, sadness and anger, addressing any deficits and distortions in thinking.' (NAS, 2011)

Such certainty of efficacy seems to simply come from a citation to Tony Attwood.

As someone who as a teen managed to narrowly avoid being diagnosed with catatonic schizophrenia, and whose 'symptoms' were brought on by extreme stress of someone on the autistic spectrum, who had also suffered psychological trauma from a road-traffic accident, I find it disturbing how a discourse of 'catatonia' is linked to autistic people. The NAS article states that the onset of catatonia can be seen via a number of symptoms: an increased slowness affecting movements and/or verbal responses, difficulty in initiating completing and inhibiting actions, increased reliance on physical or verbal prompting by others, and increased passivity and apparent lack of motivation. As an autistic person who is generally slow in movement and verbal response, who has difficulties with initiation, who may be perceived as needing verbal prompts from others, is of a generally passive temperament, and often unmotivated by phenomena outside of my areas of interest – these descriptors are not indicative of a 'mental illness', but behavioural manifestations of my autistic disposition. The report continues to state that other manifestations and 'associated behaviours' include: freezing, excitement and agitation, or a marked increase in repetitive and ritualistic behaviour. These 'manifestations' for me would signal either excitement or stress, both of which are dependent on the social environment one finds oneself in.

Another interpretation of the onset of such behaviours could be the resultant stress of being an autistic person in contemporary society, being hopelessly misunderstood by the psychiatric 'gaze'. The article does go on to acknowledge social and environmental factors, but in a way that frames the autistic person within a narrative of behavioural modification. The two-pronged attack of medical model and (cognitive-behavioural) psychological narratives has done great damage to autistic people, and takes attention away from the social conditions that autistic people find themselves in, and the disadvantaged social position such ways of thinking place autistic people in to. The narrative of 'behavioural management' also supports a damaging social ideology regarding disability.

The differences in theories regarding mental health that are expressed in these various accounts are deeply entrenched within a wider theoretical and political context. The 'treatment' of people experiencing 'problems in living' is thus set within a wider conflict in ideas, between those who wish to control and manage 'deviance from the norm', and those who question such a analysis of human subjectivities. This either/or conflict is perhaps best expressed in the debate between the 'medical' and 'social' models of disability, where attempts to split 'impairment' from 'disability' are met with resistance from both sides.

When analysing such debates, I personally take solace from an 'unusual' source, that of the 'metaphysics of quality' in the philosophical novels of Robert M Pirsig. Pirsig utilised aspects of 'Eastern' and 'Western' philosophies in an attempt to view reality in a way that went beyond the dualistic objective/subjective divide found within Western philosophy. Pirsig argued that the 'quality' of something escaped definition as its existence preceded the perceiving of it. The 'quality' of anything was thus experienced perceptually, before it could be thought about and described.

Although Pirsig suggests that such 'quality' (like the 'Tao' in Taoism) is essentially indefinable, as a means of making sense of it, he splits it into two basic forms: static (or patterned) forms of quality, and dynamic (or un-patterned) forms. As forms of 'dynamic quality' become formalised, they transform into more 'static' patterns, for example: 'bureaucracy'. A static pattern is anything that can be defined, which for the philosopher Ludwig Wittgenstein is the basis of what is 'knowable' and therefore what can be communicated, and for Pirsig, such 'patterns of static quality' are the foundations of social knowledge and culture. In this way of seeing reality though, there is not a 'duality' between static and dynamic forms of 'quality', but if one likes, a 'spectrum' of 'quality'.

Pirsig describes dynamic quality as a process that is pre-intellectual and at the 'cutting-edge' of reality, which can be immediately 'recognised', yet not 'conceptualised'. To illustrate, Pirsig gives the example of the dynamic beauty of a piece of music being recognisable, before a 'static' analysis explaining why the music is beautiful is able to be constructed. For me, the epitome of Pirsig's 'dynamic quality', is my son. My son has been variously described as 'non-verbal', 'classically autistic', and 'low functioning'. Yet his world is one of a dynamic connection to his sensory world. Sometimes attempting to force someone such as my son into more 'static' patterns of being, would make that person 'ill'. Sometimes the 'dynamic quality' that an autistic person inhabits is so chaotic, that they seek out structure and routine to impose upon it, either derived internally or from outsiders. To me, the supposed 'inflexibility' and 'rigidity' of autistic people is massively over-estimated, and mostly the misperception of someone who naturally does not inhabit such a dynamic disposition – the non-autistic 'outsider'. I think that autistic people often seem to others as 'rigid', yet internally speaking, we are often the opposite.

Pirsig argued that evolution and moral progression worked from a dynamic base to increasing forms of intellectualised static quality (for example the notion of a 'civil right'). So strangely, for someone championed by 'alternative culture', his philosophy takes on the hue of one of civilisation leading to moral advancement. This philosophy then becomes strangely reminiscent of that of Emile Durkheim's (the late 19th century sociologist), and the idea that a functional 'organic' modern society needed an element of deviance (or 'dynamism'), to provide for the 'function' of social change and transformation. Such transformations of society do not always happen peacefully though, as Marxists and others would easily point out. Such transformations of society however, are reminiscent of the 'transformations' of the individual psyche talked about by Laing and Dabrowski, and the potential for either a stronger new identity or a descent into 'dysfunctional' chaos and fragmentation. Something all these writers suggest is the inevitability of change, the need for dynamism and transformation, and yet also the negative consequences that such change can bring. The similarity between all of these phenomena is no coincidence, but represents a society dominated by an ideology of 'static' and bureaucratic rationalised social control, and a subversive multitude of dynamic narratives and practices, manifested in psychological and social diversity.

Historically, sometimes the dominant 'static' forms of authority and power lose their legitimacy and influence. Sometimes they will hold the seeds of their own destruction, and yet with new identities, social practices, and shifts in ways of thinking arriving as a result.

'If we challenge the status quo and choose not to 'blend in' but, with respect and dignity, have the courage to be who we are, then maybe we could be involved in saving the human race from one of its worst enemies – itself.' (Wendy Lawson, 2008)

References

Laing RD (1960) *The Divided Self: An existential study in sanity and madness.* Harmondsworth: Penguin.

Laing RD (1961) *The Self and Others.* London: Tavistock.

Lawson W (2008) *Concepts of Normality.* London: Jessica Kingsley.

National Autistic Society (2011) *Mental Health and Asperger Syndrome* [online]. Available at: www.autism.org.uk/working-with/health/mental-health-and-asperger-syndrome.aspx (accessed January 2011).

Pirsig RM (1974) *Zen and the Art of Motorcycle Maintenance: An inquiry into values.* London: Vertigo Press.

Pirsig RM (1991) *Lila: An inquiry into morals.* London: Black Swan.

Szasz T (1960) The Myth of Mental Illness. *American Psychologist* **15** 113–118.

Szasz T (1973) *Ceremonial Chemistry: The ritual persecution of drugs, addicts, and pushers.* New York: Syracuse University Press.

Szasz T (2009) Seven Questions for Thomas Szasz. *Psychology Today.* [online]: Available at: www.psychologytoday.com/blog/in-therapy/200901/seven-questions-thomas-szasz (accessed September 2017).

'Natures answer to over-conformity': deconstructing Pathological Demand Avoidance

This essay was first published on the 'Autism Experts' website in 2013.

Abstract

Throughout its history, autism has been primarily defined in terms of a pathologised deviancy from normative cognitive functionality, despite protestations to the contrary from autistic writers (Sinclair, 1993; Arnold, 2010; Milton, 2011). More recently however, we have witnessed the wider acceptance of a construction concerning a perceived pervasive developmental disorder known as Pathological Demand Avoidance syndrome (PDA). This conceptualisation was first formulated by Elizabeth Newson in the 1980s (PDA Contact Centre, 2012), yet more recently has been recognised by the National Autistic Society as a variant of an autistic spectrum disorder (ASD). This paper deconstructs the psychologisation of autistic agency inherent in the theory supporting PDA, through a personal reflection of an autistic activist and academic who according to such a perspective may well have met the criteria for PDA when a child. This paper concludes by arguing that the label of PDA represents the medicalising and pathologising of behaviours that from an outsider perspective seem to be differentiated from what is deemed capable by autistic people, but could be seen as the behaviours of an autistic person who has gained a modicum of normative social skills and is simply asserting their agency. By pathologising such behaviour, one could unduly be blunting attempts at autistic self-advocacy.

Me

> *'A withered boy who was so afraid, hiding from society in the shade,*
> *His solitary cries no-one did hear, his confused mind full of fear. His*
> *tortured soul locked inside, with his faded dreams that had died.'*
> (Milton, 1989)

My own journey through the world of psychiatry and psychology

As a young child I remember various GPs and teaching professionals being concerned with the question: 'What is wrong with that boy?' Early on though, my oddball quirks were put down to shyness and eccentricity, and I was diagnosed with asthma and hayfever. My first encounter with psychiatric professionals came following a road traffic accident and a court case my mother had started to claim damages through, not only for herself – she had suffered significant permanent physical injuries – but on behalf of the mental and emotional damage sustained by me and my brother, with particular attention paid to me as I seemed to have been particularly adversely affected (and I had been!). I was 11 years old at the time. During this process I was assessed by a variety of psychiatrists and psychologists, each one having a different theory as to: 'what is wrong with that boy?' These explanations ran from 'psychologically disturbed', to personality disorder and catatonic schizophrenia, with some suggesting that I had not been affected by the trauma of the accident but had an underlying condition. Following unsuccessful encounters with various counselling services I decided to avoid such professionals at all costs, with a growing fear that the 'men in white coats would come to get me'. Indeed, one could say that throughout my childhood I perfected ways of 'coping' with the imposed will of others, usually through a form of passive defiance (although not always quite so passive in my teens). Several years later after studying sociology and philosophy in an attempt to reason with the 'insanity' of the social world that I found myself in, I became a father. At the age of two my son was diagnosed with autism and severe learning difficulties. By researching this diagnosis I realised that I myself was on the autism spectrum, and was later diagnosed at the age of 36 with Asperger syndrome. Since then I went on to claim a distinction in psychology (conversion diploma) from the Open University and set about deconstructing the social construction of autism. I am now studying for my doctorate at the University of Birmingham researching the tensions between various stakeholders in the narratives regarding the education of autistic people.

Pathological Demand Avoidance (PDA)

Throughout its history, autism has been primarily defined in terms of a pathologised deviancy from normative cognitive functionality, despite protestations to the contrary from autistic writers (Sinclair, 1993, Arnold, 2010, Milton, 2011).

> '...right from the start, from the time someone came up with
> the word 'autism', the condition has been judged from the outside,
> by its appearances, and not from the inside according to how it is
> experienced.' (Williams, 1996: 14)

More recently however, we have witnessed the construction of a categorisation concerning a perceived pervasive developmental disorder known as Pathological Demand Avoidance syndrome (PDA). This conceptualisation was first formulated by Elizabeth Newson in the 1980s (PDA Contact Centre, 2012), yet more recently has been recognised by the National Autistic Society as a variant of an autistic spectrum disorder (ASD). Many of the children being diagnosed initially by the Elizabeth Newson clinic were said to display traits and characteristics of autism, yet did not show a typical presentation of 'classic' autism or Asperger syndrome, and so were often labelled with 'Atypical autism' or PDD-NOS (pervasive developmental disorder – not otherwise specified). These labels were felt to be unhelpful to the families of these children, thus spurring Newson and her followers to attempt to identify PDA as a separate syndrome.

Children characterised with PDA are believed to 'resist the ordinary demands of life' to a degree deemed pathological by clinicians (Newson *et al*, 2003). Children seen as having PDA are often described as 'Jekyll and Hyde' personalities, involving sharp mood swings, and deemed to display severe 'challenging behaviour'. As with the psychological construction of autism more generally, PDA has increasingly been identified as being produced by a combination of genetic and environmental factors which alter early brain development. Children characterised as having PDA are said to have an anxiety-led need to control their environments, possess superficial social skills, and often engage in manipulative and domineering behaviour. The criteria for PDA as devised by Newson *et al* (2003) includes:

1. Passivity in early childhood, resisting demands and missing developmental milestones.

2. Continuing to resist demands, distraction techniques, resorting to meltdowns (panic attacks) if demands are enforced.

3. Surface sociability, but apparent lack of sense of social identity, pride or shame.

4. Comfortable in role play and pretending.

5. Language delay, seemingly the result of passivity.

6. Obsessive behaviour.

7. Neurological signs – such as awkwardness, similar to autism spectrum disorders.

If one had assessed me as a child against these criteria (or for that matter as I generally present today), especially within particular contexts, I would have met them all except perhaps that of being comfortable in role play or pretending. This difference would not be enough to separate those diagnosed with Asperger syndrome, however, from those deemed to display traits of PDA when one considers successful performers or actors on the spectrum such as Paddy Consadine.

PDA is not currently recognised by either the DSM-IV or the ICD-10 nor is it under consideration for inclusion in the proposals for the new DSM-V[4]. Resistance to the inclusion of PDA into the DSM is predicated on it being a false identification of a form of attachment disorder rather than having a neurological basis (PDA Contact Centre, 2012).

Despite these conceptual issues regarding the causes of the behavioural manifestations of PDA, the label has in recent times caught the attention of many psychologists and practitioners working in the field of autism studies.

The drive behind this label to become accepted in the psychology lexicon has primarily come from Newson (Newson *et al*, 2003) herself and her successor as a clinician at the Elizabeth Newson centre: Phil Christie (2007). For Newson (2003) the main difference between those identified as having PDA rather than autism or Asperger's is that children displayed 'superficial social skills' and are 'socially manipulative'. The children often could also maintain eye contact. Other factors associated with PDA included a 'lack of self-identity', with an understanding of how others should behave, but being unable to include themselves in these expectations, often imitative of 'inappropriate behaviour' (with a recommendation to provide a 'normal' peer group to model behaviour on), and an obsessive need to dominate social interactions and for others to follow their terms, often coming across as overbearing. According to the PDA Contact Centre (2012) there are two main types of PDA: 'actively passive' and 'actively disruptive', yet with children moving between these reactions. These behaviours are seen as not involving choice or agency, but as a manifestation of not being able to cope with the 'stress of everyday demands' due to 'cognitive deficit and pathology'.

In contrast to the normative functionalist models of mind and behaviour that are demonstrated in the vast majority of literature regarding autism and related pervasive developmental disorders, autistic self-advocates often remark on how autism can be better understood as a cognitive difference or diversity, and that the breakdown in communication and empathy impacts of both parties (Sinclair, 1993; Milton, 2012a). Taking an interactionist or post-structural approach to social relations, it is quite bizarre to

---

4   It was not included.

speak of someone being able to possess definable social 'skills' which are not dependent on a multitude of social influences, simply not attended to by the individualising approach of cognitive functionalism. Thus, in this conceptualisation, what can be deemed appropriate, challenging, overbearing and so on are negotiated positionalities. The labelling of the expressions of autistic agency as pathological is in itself disempowering.

According to research quoted by the PDA Contact Centre (2012), there are statistically significant differences between PDA and autism/Asperger syndrome, in that PDA children are less likely to:

- have caused anxiety to parents before 18 months of age

- show stereotypical motor mannerisms

- show (or have shown) echolalia or pronoun reversal

- show speech anomalies in terms of pragmatics

- show (or have shown) tiptoe walking

- show compulsive adherence to routines.

This list includes a contradiction, however, in that children who are meant to show 'soft' neurological signs of awkwardness or clumsiness are also statistically significantly less likely to walk on tiptoes. As someone who often paces or walks on tiptoes in order to gain feedback of where they are in their environment, this seems to be highly unlikely to be such a significant difference between those potentially characterised as having PDA or Asperger syndrome. Along with this list, there is also one regarding attributes found to be statistically significant in terms of regularity within the group of children thus characterised:

- Resist demands obsessively.

- Be socially manipulative.

- Show normal eye contact

- Show excessive lability of mood and impulsivity.

- Show social mimicry (includes gestures and personal style).

- Show role play (more extended and complete than mimicry).

- Show other types of symbolic play.

- Be female (50%).

If one were to apply these criteria to me, it would be hard to characterise my actions as 'manipulative', and I am certainly not good at, or motivated by, social mimicry or role play. Newson *et al* (2003) and Christie (2007) would suggest that these differences are definably different to the traits found in autistic people, yet as said earlier, there are successful performers and actors that are on the spectrum who do display these skills. When considering such a distinction, Christie (2007) suggests that it is an important sub-type to distinguish, due to the idea that children with PDA do not respond well to traditional behavioural techniques deemed successful with those on the autism spectrum. The obvious weakness with this argument is that such techniques are not 'successful' according to many autistic people either (Dawson, 2004; Milton, 2012b).

It is also suggested that children displaying PDA are more likely to become obsessed with particular individuals or relationships and as utilising bizarre content in language use, conceived as to be more common than in autism, due to an interest in fantasy. Similar attributes however have been made regarding women on the autism spectrum (Simone, 2010) and it is interesting to note that PDA is considered to be affecting an equal number of males and females. Could it just be the case that PDA is an unnecessary extra arbitrary line in the sand?

> '*Extremes of any combination come to be seen as "psychiatric deviance". In the argument presented here, where disorder begins is entirely down to social convention, and where one decides to draw the line across the spectrum.*' (Milton, 1999 – spectrum referring to the 'human spectrum of dispositional diversity')

The major reason for the growing interest in PDA has, according to Christie (2007), been in the sense of recognition expressed by both parents and professionals of the behavioural profile as described by Newson *et al* (2003) and how different it is conceived to be from conventional understandings of ASD. It is argued here that such statements are based on flawed, misguided theories regarding what autism is (Milton, 2012c), and thus the supposed differences between these categories begin to evaporate under closer inspection. Wing and Gould (2002) contend that PDA is not a separate syndrome and that the behavioural features portrayed in the PDA children can be found within individuals with a diagnosis of ASD. Having said this, they also consider PDA research to be 'innovative' and clinically useful.

> '*Individuals with PDA tend to have over-active imaginations as opposed to under-active, and this clearly sets them apart from Wing's description of the autistic Triad of Impairments.*' (PDA Contact Centre, 2012)

The above statement reifies the idea that autistic people lack imagination, and that someone displaying imagination in some external sense could not possibly be autistic and thus PDA would be a more accurate descriptor. This is, however, a misinterpretation, in my view, of the autistic mind-set where the apparent rigidity of many on the spectrum can be due to a number of factors, from monotropic focus (Murray *et al*, 2005) to stress and overload (Milton, 2012c) or a need to control one's external environment (which is exactly the same reasons purported to be creating an avoidance of demands in descriptions of PDA). A major difficulty in suggesting that a behavioural manifestation is not autistic, is that to make such a statement one would have to have a good idea of what autism is, and this should be anything but a presumed given, considering the lack of clarity and explanatory value the dominant psychological theories contain (Milton, 2011).

> *'It is important to remember that PDA is not caused by a person's upbringing or their social circumstances and it is not the fault of the parents or the individual with the condition.'*
> (Christie & Duncan, 2012)

There is simply not enough evidence to support a claim such as this, especially when there are similar traits associated with both developmental and attachment disorders. It is more than possible that autistic people can be traumatised by social relationships, and by negating such factors as ever having a causative association with avoidance behaviours could be potentially negligent. Unfortunately current theories regarding attachment and trauma are not much more coherent than that regarding PDA.

Educational discourse regarding PDA children

> *'...many parents describe their child as working harder to avoid the demand than she would have done by accepting it. Whatever the child's intellectual level ... educational support will need to be geared to helping the child to tolerate "being educated" to the greatest degree possible, in order at least to approach her potential.'* (PDA Contact Centre, 2012)

In this statement, the PDA Contact Centre (2012) equates 'being educated' with conformity to non-autistic hegemonic practices. The notion that a child on the autism spectrum would have to work less to comply with demands than to reject them displays a total lack of empathy with many an autistic perspective. As a case in point, I was once asked to summarise autism in three words, the answer I gave was:

'Natures answer to over-conformity…'.

According to the PDA Contact Centre (2012) there are three main educational needs that practitioners working with such children need to consider:

- Keeping the child on task for a substantial period of the day.
- Ensuring that what she appears to be learning is actually absorbed and retained.
- Ensuring that a minimal degree of disruption to other children takes place, and trying to create positive peer relationships despite the resentment such disruption can cause in other children. Sometimes this will include the need to keep other children physically safe.

Such an educational agenda applied to any child, I would consider woefully teacher-led, as it does not highlight at any point the building of a relationship or an attempt to understand the educational context from the position of the learner. The learner's role in this context is simply to stay on the task as envisaged by the non-autistic adult.

'However, a mainstream school is appropriate wherever possible, as PDA children are socially imitative and therefore good normative models are important.' (PDA Contact, 2012)

The above quote belies a damaging ideology that has been embedded within behaviourist models of autism since the writings of Lovaas (1987) in that the company of other autistic or neuro-divergent individuals would be a negative influence on one another by modelling inappropriate behaviours. In the mind of this autistic person however, nothing has been more disabling than being isolated from those with similar dispositions (Milton, 2012b).

Christie (2007) suggests that diagnosis of PDA should help to better understand an individual and to use that understanding to help 'formulate more effective forms of intervention and provision'. As with most literature regarding autism, the emphasis is thus on intervening with the perceived deviant disorder in a remedial effort to normalise behaviour.

> '...many of the generally accepted strategies that are advocated
> for working for children with autism and Asperger's syndrome
> were not proving successful for children with PDA; an altogether
> different emphasis was required ... The use of structure, routine and
> behavioural principles of reward that are usually effective for children
> with autism or Asperger's syndrome are rarely so for children with
> PDA.' (Christie, 2007)

Although somewhat redeeming this account by reminding readers that no
one set of guidelines is applicable to all on the autism spectrum, Christie
(2007) falls foul of assuming that behaviourist principles as applied to
autistic people are effective in the first place, ignoring the discourse of
autistic writers which are often quite to the contrary (Dawson, 2004;
Milton, 2012b). Despite recommending the building up of trust and mutual
relationships with key workers and the 'Circles of Friends' technique,
the advice offered by Christie (2007) holds conformity to appropriate
normative behaviour as the ultimate outcome to work toward, conformity
and adaptation to the demands of the non-autistic world rather than a truly
mutual exchange.

> 'People with PDA tend to respond much better to a more indirect
> and negotiative style that allows them to feel in control.' (Christie &
> Duncan, 2012).

Such an approach would also be recommended with autistic people more
generally (Milton, 2012c), yet the manner of such negotiation would be
dependent on each person and context, although sometimes it is beneficial
to actually give children (autistic or not) the power and control to make
their own autonomous decisions from time to time. This begs the question:
exactly who has a 'pathological' need to control whom?

The construction of PDA can thus be seen as an emblem of
contemporary biopower in action (Foucault, 1973; Finkelstein, 1997),
based upon the construction of self in terms of the discourses of cognitive
and developmental psychology reproduced in educational ideology and
practice, with those so labelled subjected to a pathologising gaze and
modified to meet idealised standards. Such a construction can be seen in
its contemporary social nexus as a reaction to individuals seen as a risk to
productivity and conformity to normative standards, in need of 'discipline
and control', a not-so 'docile body' to be transformed and modified so it
becomes as such.

Conclusion

In the eyes of many psychologists, educational practitioners, and parents, there are many people who would fit the criteria for PDA, however that does not mean the conceptualisation of what is causing such behaviours is at all well understood. The PDA narrative presents what is perfectly rational behaviour from the viewpoint of the autistic person displaying it when faced with highly stressful situations, not as a consequence of 'choice' (whatever that may be) but as a pathological response. It is deemed pathological due the distaste of those doing the perceiving and their idealisation of cultural and psychological norms.

The PDA narrative suggests that those who gain some social interaction skills and assert their needs through avoidance of imposed demands are pathological. In essence, such protests are perceived as the fault of pathology inherent in the individual mind rather than a conflicting interaction (much like 'theory of mind'). It will no doubt lead to treatments that try and stop such behaviours (which could be read as a form of self-advocacy and the gaining of skills). Such behaviours arise from any number of transactions between the individual and environment. The avoidance of demands is interactional in nature, and much like a lack of social reciprocity cannot be located solely in the mind of any one individual (Milton, 2012a).

The label of PDA represents the medicalising and pathologising of behaviours that from an outsider perspective seem to be differentiated from what is deemed capable by autistic people, but could be seen as the behaviours of an autistic person who has gained a modicum of normative social skills and is simply asserting their agency. By pathologising such behaviour, one could unduly be blunting attempts at autistic self-advocacy. Part of this misperception is due to the application of a deficit model of autism that considers autistic people as incapable of displaying social agency. As with other labels in the psychologisation of human social life, it is a descriptive construction from a medicalised pathologising functionalist discourse, yet even less than other labels it does not signpost practitioners to the needs of the person, but to the needs of those around them. One could even argue that there is a struggle for power embedded in the discourse, in which one could question who it is who needs to control whom, an incidence of biopower in action.

Distortion

> 'As the final door begins to close, we make do with what our leaders impose. What are they implying, what is the message that is underlying? We are polluted by this infestation, I need an outlet for my frustration. I don't want to comply, and I have no need to justify.' (Milton, 1989)

A point of clarification

At the time of writing this essay there was much contention as to whether 'PDA' should be considered a variant or sub-category of autism, a separate definable condition, or a particular framing of behaviours often seen to be displayed by autistic people. There would now seem to be something of a consensus forming around the latter description within the field. This however still leaves the problem of the medicalised and pathologising narrative and theory that accompanies a diagnosis of autism with a 'PDA profile', as well as the diagnostic overlap with reactions to trauma or attachment issues. Recently, this essay came under criticism from advocates who have found personal use from the term, or whom identify themselves with the profile. This criticism included a misinterpretation of my intention in drawing attention to this diagnostic overlap. The intention here was not to give licence to practitioners to mother blame for a child being autistic and (rationally) avoiding 'demands'.

There are now a growing number of accounts from autistic people regarding the multiple effects of stress and trauma in their lives, which in some cases can exacerbate reactions such as avoidance. In the vast majority of cases, this trauma comes from navigating a social world which is anything but 'autism-friendly'. More often than not, it is our parents who are our greatest advocates, often in the face of their own social stigmatisation and exclusion. The frequency of intentional parental child abuse is minute in comparison to the numbers of autistic people, and yet mothers in particular are often blamed, when it is often services that are failing, and in some cases being neglectful (see later chapter entitled 'Moments in time'). For autistic people, it is often the assumptions of ill-informed practitioners that we need safeguarding from. What is for certain is that some high quality research is needed to look into all of these issues in more depth.

References

American Psychiatric Association (1994) *Diagnostic and statistical manual of mental disorders (4th Edition) (DSM-IV)*. Washington DC: APA.

Arnold L (2010) *The Medium is the Message* [online]. London: University College London.

Christie P (2007) *The Distinctive Clinical and Educational Needs of Children with Pathological Demand Avoidance Syndrome: Guidelines for Good Practice* [online]. Available at: www.aettraininghubs.org.uk/wp-content/uploads/2012/05/5.2-strategies-for-teaching-pupils-with-PDA.pdf (accessed October 2017).

Chirstie P & Duncan M (2012) *Pathological Demand Avoidance* [online]. www.autism.org.uk/about/what-is/pda.aspx (accessed October 2017).

Dawson M (2004) *The Misbehaviour of Behaviourists: Ethical challenges to the autism-ABA industry,* [online]. Available at: www.sentex.net/~nexus23/naa_aba.html (accessed September 2017).

Finkelstein V (1997) Chic outrage and body politics. In: K Davis (ed.) *Embodied Practices: Feminist perspectives on the body* pp.150–169. London: Sage.

Foucault M (1973) *Madness and Civilisation: A history of insanity in the age of reason* (trans. R Howard). New York: Vintage.

Lovaas O (1987) Behavioural treatment and normal educational and intellectual functioning in young autistic children. *Journal of Consulting and Clinical Psychology* **55** 3–9.

Milton D (1989) *Chapters of the Lifehouse* [collected poems]. Unpublished.

Milton D (1999) *The Rise of Psychopharmacology*. Masters Degree Essay: University of London.

Milton D (2011) Who am I meant to be?: in search of a psychological model of autism from the viewpoint of an 'insider'. *Critical Autism Seminar* 18/01/11. Sheffield: Sheffield Hallam University.

Milton D (2012a) On the ontological status of autism: the double empathy problem. *Disability and Society* **27** (6).

Milton D (2012b) The Normalisation Agenda and the Psycho-Emotional Disablement of Autistic People. *Critical Disability Studies Conference* 13/09/12. Lancaster University.

Milton D (2012c) *So what exactly is autism?* [online]. Available at: www. aettraininghubs.org.uk/wp-content/uploads/2012/08/1_So-what-exactly-is-autism.pdf (accessed October 2017).

Murray D, Lesser M & Lawson W (2005) Attention, monotropism and the diagnostic criteria for autism. *Autism* **9** (2) 136–156.

Newson E, Le Marechal K & David C (2003) Pathological Demand Avoidance syndrome: a necessary distinction within the pervasive developmental disorders. *Archives of Disease in Childhood* **88** 595–600.

PDA Contact Centre (2012) [online]: www.pdacontact.org.uk/frames/index.html, [Accessed 5th October 2012].

Simone R (2010) *Aspergirls: Empowering females with asperger syndrome*. London: Jessica Kingsley.

Sinclair J (1993) *Don't Mourn For Us* [online]. Available at: www.autreat.com/dont_mourn.html (accessed September 2017).

Williams D (1996) *Autism: An inside out approach*. London: Jessica Kingsley

Wing L & Gould J (2002) *Pathological Demand Avoidance*. London: National Autistic Society.

World Health Organisation (1992) *The tenth revision of the international classification of diseases and related health problems (ICD-10)*. Geneva: WHO.

Impaired compared to what? Embodiment and diversity

This essay was first delivered as a presentation for the Mad Studies and Neurodiversity Symposium on 17th June 2015.

> *'Extremes of any combination come to be seen as "psychiatric deviance". In the argument presented here, where disorder begins is entirely down to social convention, and where one decides to draw the line across the spectrum.'* (Milton, 1999 – spectrum referring to the 'human spectrum of dispositional diversity')

Ever since I developed a personal memory of self, I have lived at the intersection between disability and madness. Following a road-traffic accident in 1984 my mother sustained significant long-term injuries, whilst I suffered significant psychological trauma. In the years ahead, due to a court case following the accident, I visited a number of psychiatrists, who each had their own theory as to explain my odd behaviour. Following these patronising and intimidating encounters I planned to create as much space between me and such professionals as I could, yet also began a personal journey of discovery that led me toward philosophy and the social sciences. By the mid-1990s I had discovered the work of radical psychiatrists and, by the late 1990s, the social model of disability. Both these influences helped me to begin revaluating my own disposition in relation to others.

> *'The box most applicable to my perceptions of selfhood in Kramer's analysis, is that of the "socially isolative schizoid", which to me underlies a belittling of "abnormal" dispositions.'* (Milton, 1999)

At the time I had been influenced by the work of Pierre Bourdieu and his notions of 'habitus' and 'disposition' and how a person is shaped within their social environments. The notion of disposition also for me encapsulated a feeling of embodied personhood. Yet my experiences of life and the fragmented disposition I embodied did not seem to be much like that of many others I had come across in life, and from such a perspective I saw a great diversity in the way people are shaped biologically and discursively, and a strong rejection of normative notions of what an 'ideal person' should be like.

In 2005 my son was diagnosed as autistic. This began another journey that led me to being diagnosed as on the autistic spectrum myself in 2009 and that there existed a whole 'neurodiversity movement' and paradigm for thinking and talking about autism, one that perhaps unsurprisingly, was not so different from my own.

So, given the influence that the social model of disability had on my own thinking and sense of selfhood, why do I wish to problematise the notion of 'impairment'? First, let me make clear that I in no way mean to negate the diversity of human experience and embodiment, quite the opposite. Second, I in no way wish to diminish the importance of social model theorists. However, the notion of 'impairment' has normative connotations and at least has been used to the detriment of autistic people. When one looks at the idea of biological impairment, there is always a comparison to be made, and too often something idealised as 'better' or more 'functional' in some way. Impairment has become a phrase used to describe abstract notions of deficit compared to a statistical average. When as an adult I was diagnosed as autistic, an extensive history of childhood development was taken, no doubt making comparisons to what was deemed 'typical' child development. Such comparisons are taken in part so that adaptations and interventions can be recommended with the goal of normative remediation of said deficits. When looked at in terms of dispositional diversity however, remediation is removed as a primary goal, as there is not a normative comparison to be made nor idealisation of a normative way of being. Of course, accepting and celebrating one's disposition when others may treat you as a stigmatised outsider is no easy task, yet a measure of solidarity I believe is possible, as the personal troubles that I have experienced may not be too dissimilar to others involved in this conference.

Reference

Milton D (1999) *The Rise of Psychopharmacology.* Masters Degree essay: University of London.

Part two:
A mismatch of salience

In this section, three chapters are presented which are fundamental to my own theorising regarding autism. The first chapter in this section was my first academic publication in a journal and outlined the concept of the 'double empathy problem'. This concept originated in my own explanations to parents of, and practitioners working with, autistic children regarding the mutual incomprehension and breakdown in communication that often occurs when autistic and non-autistic people interact. The development of the concept came in part as a riposte to the dominance of the one-sided 'theory of mind' hypothesis within the field of autism studies. The deeper roots of this concept however, are embedded within a philosophy of 'dispositional diversity' that I had been developing since the 1990s. The second chapter in this section gives an overview of some of the influences on this philosophy, particularly in the fields of interpretive and phenomenological sociology and social psychology. This chapter utilises the term 'disposition', not in the sense of 'innate characteristics', but as a term that both entails biological affordances and social influences on the formation of notions of self more akin to the work of Pierre Bourdieu. The final chapter in this section re-examines the double empathy problem through the concept of 'interactional expertise' as developed by Harry Collins and Rob Evans. It is from the work of Collins and Evans where I first came across the term 'mismatched salience', to which I owe the title of this collection, and which perhaps best summarises my theorising regarding autistic interactions with others. In the conclusion to this essay, I argue that at least some interactional expertise must be possible between autistic and non-autistic people. Since these essays were published, there have been a small number of research reports that would seem to at least in part support the theory of the double empathy problem (references listed below). It is my hope, however, that these issues are investigated further in the future.

References

Edey R, Cook J, Brewer R, Johnson MH, Bird G & Press C (2016) Interaction takes two: Typical adults exhibit mind-blindness towards those with autism spectrum disorder. *Journal of Abnormal Psychology* **125** (7) 879.

Gernsbacher M, Stevenson J & Dern S (2017) Specificity, contexts, and reference groups matter when assessing autistic traits. *PloS one* **12** (2).

Heasman B & Gillespie A (2017) Perspective-taking is two-sided: misunderstandings between people with Asperger's syndrome and their family members. *Autism.* First published date: July-07-2017. 10.1177/1362361317708287.

Sasson N, Faso D, Nugent J, Lovell S, Kennedy D & Grossman R (2017) Neurotypical peers are less willing to interact with those with autism based on thin slice judgments. *Scientific Reports* **7** 40700.

Sheppard E, Pillai D, Wong GTL, Ropar D & Mitchell P (2016) How easy is it to read the minds of people with autism spectrum disorder? *Journal of autism and Developmental Disorders* **46** (4) 1247–1254.

On the ontological status of autism: the 'double empathy problem'

This essay is derived in part from an article published in Disability & Society on 16 Aug 2012, available online: http://wwww.tandfonline.com/ http://dx.doi.org/10.1080/09687599.2012.710008

Abstract

In recent decades there has been much debate over the ontological status of autism and other neurological 'disorders', diagnosed by behavioural indicators, and theorised primarily within the field of cognitive neuroscience and psychological paradigms. Such cognitive-behavioural discourses abstain from acknowledging the universal issue of relationality and interaction in the formation of a contested and constantly reconstructed social reality, produced through the agency of its 'actors'. The nature of these contested interactions will be explored in this article through the use of the term the 'double empathy problem', and how such a rendition produces a critique of autism being defined as a deficit in 'theory of mind', re-framing such issues as a question of reciprocity and mutuality. In keeping with other autistic self-advocates, this piece will refer to 'autistic people', and 'those who identify as on the autism spectrum', rather than 'people with autism'.

Introduction

> **Socrates:** *…Can you point out any compelling rhetorical reason why he should have put his arguments together in the order that he has?*
> **Phaedrus:** *You do me too much honour if you suppose that I am capable of divining his motives so exactly.*
> (Plato, 1973, 78)

In recent decades there has been much debate over the ontological status of autism and other neurological 'disorders', diagnosed by behavioural indicators, and theorised primarily within the field of cognitive neuroscience and psychological paradigms. The triad of dominant theories includes theory of mind deficit, executive dysfunction, and weak central coherence theory, as well as behavioural diagnosis and behavioural psychological intervention paradigms; all position autism as a neurological disorder, a pathological deviance from expected functional stages of development. This approach, when applied to the education of those diagnosed, becomes a 'treatment programme' of modifying the 'autistic person' as 'best one can' to fit in with the mainstream culture of society. Such views are informed by research that champions the use of the randomised controlled trial, yet discounts the subjective experiences of those who identify as being on the autism spectrum themselves as worthy of rigorous academic study. Such cognitive-behavioural discourses abstain from acknowledging the universal issue of relationality and interaction in the formation of a contested and constantly reconstructed social reality, produced through the agency of its 'actors'. The nature of these contested interactions will be explored in this article through the use of the term the 'double empathy problem' (Milton 2011a), and how such a rendition produces a critique of autism being defined as a deficit in 'theory of mind' and social interaction, re-framing such issues as a question of reciprocity and mutuality.

Assumptions of social relationality

The inability to 'read' the subtext of a social situation is often deemed to be a major feature of those diagnosed as being on the autism spectrum, yet it is suggested here that social subtext is never fully given as a set of a priori circumstances, but is actively constructed by social agents engaged in material and mental production. There is a tendency in the application of positivist methodologies in cognitive psychology and science to incorrectly assume that there is a set of definable social norms and rules that exist for people to follow. This ideology is also supported more explicitly by functionalist sociologists. This is not the philosophy propounded by those of a phenomenological or ethnomethodological persuasion, however. The 'theory of mind' and 'empathy' so lauded in normative psychological models of human interaction refers to the ability a 'non-autistic spectrum' (non-AS) individual has to assume understandings of the mental states and motives of other people. When such 'empathy' is applied toward an 'autistic person', however, it is often wildly inaccurate in its measure. Such attempts are often felt as invasive, imposing and threatening by an 'autistic person', especially when protestations to the contrary are ignored by the non-AS person doing the 'empathising'.

> *'The "double empathy problem": a disjuncture in reciprocity*
> *between two differently disposed social actors which becomes more*
> *marked the wider the disjuncture in dispositional perceptions of the*
> *lifeworld – perceived as a breach in the "natural attitude" of what*
> *constitutes "social reality" for "non-autistic spectrum" people and*
> *yet an everyday and often traumatic experience for "autistic people".*
> (Author's concept and definition)

To expand on the above definition, the 'double empathy problem' refers to a breach in the 'natural attitude' (Garfinkel, 1967) that occurs between people of different dispositional outlooks and personal conceptual understandings when attempts are made to communicate meaning. In a sense it is a 'double problem' because both people experience it, and so it is not a singular problem located in any one person. Rather, it is based in the social interaction between two differently disposed social actors, the disjuncture being more severe for the non-autistic disposition as it is experienced as unusual, while for the 'autistic person' it is a common experience (Milton 2011b). The 'empathy' problem being a 'two-way street' has been mentioned by both 'autistic writers' (Sinclair, 1993) and non-AS writers alike (Hacking, 2009), yet, despite such protestations, the 'lack of theory of mind' myth persists.

The stigma of being 'othered' and the normalisation agenda

To be defined as abnormal in society is often conflated with being perceived as 'pathological' in some way and to be socially stigmatised, shunned and sanctioned. Then, if there is a breakdown in interaction, or indeed a failed attempt to align toward expressions of meaning, a person who sees their interactions as 'normal' and 'correct' can denigrate those who act or are perceived of as 'different' (Tajfel & Turner, 1979). If one can apply a label on the 'other' locating the problem in them, it also resolves the applier of the label's 'natural attitude' of responsibility in their own perceptions and the breach is healed perceptually, but not for the person who has been 'othered' (Said, 1978).

Internalised oppression and psycho-emotional disablement

The imposition of one's views upon another and the subsequent internalisation of this view can be seen to be a form of internalised oppression, where the negative connotations of the normative model of pathological difference become a self-fulfilling prophecy (Becker, 1963), leading to a self-imposed psycho-emotional disablement (Reeve, 2011). For those who resist, such self-identifications and attempts to normalise – however 'well intentioned' – are experienced as an 'invasion' of the 'autistic' 'lifeworld' by people wanting to modify one's behaviour to suit their purposes and not one's own (Milton & Lyte, 2012).

Autism and knowledge production

Although, compared with many categorisations of disability, autism has attained a great deal more public attention and one could say that the label has become a fetishised commodity and even a global industry (Mallet, 2011), it is an industry that silences the autistic voice from any participation, other than in the form of a tokenistic gesture. Therefore, far from owning the means of mental production about one's own culture, the 'autistic individual' often becomes the 'product' of the industry, the 'thing' that is 'intervened' with. 'Services' are provided for the carers of 'autistic people', often with little attention given to the needs of the 'autistic person' as they perceive them to be. Autism is not just an 'invisible disability' to many in terms of a behavioural definition; the 'autistic voice' is made 'invisible' within the current culture of how knowledge is produced about 'autistic people', often excluding empowered 'autistic advocates' from the process.

Implications for service providers

There is a spectrum in theory and practice more generally regarding service provision for 'autistic people'. At one end are those adhering to techniques of behavioural modification, so that children are socialised into what are deemed appropriate behaviours of socially functional future roles. At the other extreme of this spectrum is an ethos of interactive mutuality concerned with the empowerment of individuals and communities, where dominance and imposition of authority are seen as 'dysfunctional'. Expressions of these extremes could be said to be found more frequently in discourses regarding best educational practice for 'autistic people', ranging from the efforts of the Lovaas model of applied behavioural analysis through to child-focused and democratic educational ideological preferences. These narratives and practices can be said to be embedded within the wider discursive debate that exists between the medical and social models of disability as played out in the field of autism. It is the view of this author that there is an increasing complacency around the idea that lead professionals and practitioners have a good understanding of what 'good autism practice' entails; for me this is an ongoing imperfect process of interaction and should never be seen as a given.

Conclusion

The lack of 'social insight' seen to be manifested in the actions of 'autistic people' is both biologically and socially derived, and yet is also historically and culturally situated in discourse. The experience of a lack of realisation or the lack of insight is a very common one in social interactions of many varieties, however, and leads to the 'double empathy problem' between differently disposed social actors. Such divergences of perception are inevitable to a greater or lesser extent. So it is true that autistic people often lack insight about non-AS perceptions and culture, yet it is equally the case that non-AS people lack insight into the minds and culture of 'autistic people', or that they may lack social insight in other social situations due to an easily repaired natural attitude, and the aligning tendencies of their peers. One could say that many autistic people have indeed gained a greater level of insight into non-AS society, and more than vice versa, perhaps due to the need to survive and potentially thrive in a non-AS culture. Conversely, the non-AS person has no pertinent personal requirement to understand the mind of the 'autistic person' unless closely related socially in some way.

In analysing the interactions that 'autistic people' have with the wider population, it is easy to problematise the definition of autism as a 'social deficit' located within an individual's mind. Differences in neurology may well produce differences in sociality, but not a 'social deficit' as compared with an idealised normative view of social reality. Such definitions may help to signpost disability support services, but they are no way of defining autism in any kind of holistic sense.

> **Socrates:** *But suppose the words used are 'just' and 'good'. Don't we then go each his own way, and find ourselves in disagreement with ourselves as well as with each other?*
> **Phaedrus:** *Undoubtedly.*
> (Plato, 1973, 77)

References

Becker H (1963) *Outsiders.* New York: The Free Press.

Garfinkel H (1967) *Studies in Ethnomethodology*. Englewood Cliffs, NJ: Prentice Hall.

Hacking I (2009) Autistic autobiography. *Philosophical Transactions of the Royal Society: Biological Sciences* **364** (1522) 1467–73.

Mallet R (2011) *Buying new normals?: when impairment categories become commodities.* Paper presented at the *Theorising Normalcy and the Mundane 2nd International Conference*, September 14–15, in Manchester Metropolitan University, UK.

Milton D (2011a) *Who am I meant to be?: In search of a psychological model of autism from the viewpoint of an 'insider'.* Paper presented at the *Critical Autism Seminar*, January 18, in Sheffield Hallam University, UK.

Milton D (2011b) *Filling in the gaps: a micro-sociological analysis of autism.* Paper presented at the *Theorising Normalcy and the Mundane 2nd International Conference*, September 14–15, in Manchester Metropolitan University, UK.

Milton D & Lyte (2012) The normalisation agenda and the psycho-emotional disablement of autistic people. *Autonomy: The Journal of Critical Interdisciplinary Autism Studies* **1** (1).

Plato (1973) *Phaedrus and Letters VII and VIII.* Trans. W. Hamilton. London: Penguin.

Reeve D (2011) *Ableism within disability studies: the myth of the reliable and contained body.* Paper presented at the *Theorising Normalcy and the Mundane 2nd International Conference*, September 14-15, in Manchester Metropolitan University, UK.

Said E (1978) *Orientalism.* London: Vintage Press.

Sinclair J (1993) *Don't mourn for us.* www.autreat.com/dont_mourn.html (accessed September 2017).

Tajfel H & J Turner (1979) An integrative theory of intergroup conflict. In: *Critical Readings in Social Psychology.* D Langbridge and S Taylor (Eds) 136–147. Milton Keynes: Open University.

Embodied sociality and the conditioned relativism of dispositional diversity

This article was first published in the Autonomy journal **1**(3) *in 2014.*

Abstract

This paper explores the concepts of embodiment (Merleau-Ponty, 1945), as well as those of conditioned relativism and dispositional diversity as first devised by the papers author some 15 years ago as an undergraduate student, and applies them to debates regarding neurodiversity. These concepts were devised by the author many years prior to being diagnosed as being on the autistic spectrum, having been previously assessed as suffering from a number of mental illnesses by a number of psychiatrists in his youth. Drawing upon Marxist and phenomenological theories in particular, these concepts are explained through an eclectic citation of references ranging from Lao Tsu to Jimi Hendrix. These philosophical/sociological conceptions will be contrasted with those of others within the neurodiversity movement as a way of highlighting the need for autistic solidarity and the disabling effects of being isolated from others of similar disposition. It is hoped that through this overview, a theoretical account of autistic difference being a normal part of the diversity characteristic of all nature, and thus hopefully dislodging the hegemonic dominance of what constitutes normalcy.

Introduction

> **Socrates:** *...there are two types of madness, one arising from human disease, the other when heaven sets us free from established convention.*
> **Phaedrus:** *Agreed.*
> (Plato, 1973, 80-81)

Throughout human history there has been narratives regarding madness and psychological abnormality. The above quote from the dialogues of Plato sets out two very differing narratives however, that have persisted to this day. The former describes madness in terms of an illness, a disease that blights the mental faculties of those who suffer from it. The latter a far more positive view of mental abnormality that frames such deviance as a setting free from established convention. In the dialogue, Socrates and Phaedrus separate these two narratives out to define two differing types of mental abnormality, one good and one not. Yet in the narratives surrounding mental and neurological diversities today similar narratives abound of both kinds regarding the same socially constructed conditions.

This paper charts the development of a philosophy regarding the dispositional diversity of human agency that originated in my own undergraduate study some 15 years ago. As a teenager I had been labelled with a number of psychiatric conditions, all of which did not sit well with my own personal experiences and understandings. This led to an aversion of the psychiatric profession, yet also the beginning of a search to understand why I felt so socially different. This search led me to the study of philosophy and sociology, where I began to build theories regarding dispositional diversity and the conditioned relativism of human agency.

> *'The box most applicable to my perceptions of selfhood in Kramer's (1994) analysis, is that of the "socially isolative schizoid", which to me underlies a belittling of "abnormal" dispositions.'* (Milton, 1999)

It was during this period that I also studied the works of radical psychiatrists and work regarding the social model of disability. These ideas were brought sharply to focus, however, when my son was diagnosed as autistic some years ago. In researching autism it became apparent that I myself could be considered as on the autism spectrum and I was later diagnosed in 2009 at the age of 36. In the years before my diagnosis I had become increasingly aware that I was not alone in my philosophical ruminations, as to my surprise there was an entire neurodiversity movement already in existence.

Drawing upon Marxist and phenomenological theories in particular, this paper explores the concepts of dispositional diversity and conditioned relativism. These philosophical/sociological conceptions will be contrasted with those of others within the neurodiversity movement as a way of highlighting the need for autistic solidarity and the disabling effects of being isolated from others of similar disposition. It is hoped that through this overview, a theoretical account of autism and neurodiversity will be presented.

Conditioned relativism and dispositional diversity

'Men make their own history, but they do not make it just as they please. The tradition of all the dead generations weighs like a nightmare on the brain of the living.' (Marx, 1852/1970:15)

It has long been recognised that people are both materially and discursively produced and conditioned within a historical and cultural context. Yet such assertions can also lead to a philosophy of mind that is purely deterministic, running contrary to the liberal ideals of free will, choice, rights and responsibilities. According to the theory of conditioned relativism, unconstrained free will is a myth, with every entity being somewhat interconnected with the material and social nexus which produced them. The appearance of a unified self with a coherent consciousness able to freely act being an illusion created by each embodied person being conditioned uniquely and relativistically. Despite the entity of a self being entirely dependent on the material and social environment it finds itself in, the emergent property of consciousness is, within this conceptualisation, uniquely dependent on the somatic affordances (physical limitations) of a physical brain. Thus social agents are constructed in a unique way, yet one which is fully configured within a material and social environment. An entity dependent on the social for survival and yet is an active agent within it. Although all humans are conditioned in this way, each occupies a unique trajectory in their development, each building their own experiences and perceptions of social life and even their use of language. Language may contain what is communicable, yet much meaning is lost in translation (Milton, 2012). Such issues are further contorted by social positionality and relations of power. The social perception of the socially alienated outsider (Becker, 1963) has long been of issue in social theorising and is reflected by attempts to both normalise populations deemed as deviant, and in reactions of insider standpoint epistemology, concerns regarding reflection in practice and on positionality in research, feminist concerns of situated knowledge, and more recently the expressions of neurodiverse activists.

'Extremes of any combination come to be seen as "psychiatric deviance". In the argument presented here, where disorder begins is entirely down to social convention, and where one decides to draw the line across the spectrum.' (Milton, 1999 – spectrum referring to the human spectrum of dispositional diversity)

The outcome of the conditioned relativism of human embodied sociality creates a diversity of dispositions and developmental trajectories. Thus in the formulation, there is no neuro-typical to deviate from other than an idealised fantastical construction of Galtonian inspired psychological measurement. The above quote suggests that there are arbitrary lines drawn in the sand between what constitutes normality and psychiatric (or indeed neurological) deviance from often arbitrary measurements comparing the development of children against a flawed theory of stages and milestones.

Trait theories of personality

Throughout history, personality was conceived of in terms of types, perhaps the earliest being those of Hippocrates in Ancient Greece, who divided people into categories: melancholic, choleric, phlegmatic and sanguine; based upon a scientifically naive notion of an excess or lack of bodily humours. Butt (2007) explains how contemporary theories regarding individual differences in personality grew from three dominant psychological traditions: experimental, psychometric and clinical. All of these strands of thought are interested in the individual differences that people express, in terms of behaviour and what is commonly perceived as personality. The experimental tradition, often argued to be the dominant one within 20th century psychology began with behaviourist theories, before being largely surpassed by cognitive theories in the latter half of the century. The psychometric tradition originated in attempts to measure cognitive abilities such as intelligence, establishing traits (ways in which individuals could be said to differ from one another).

Trait theories are exemplified in the work of Eysenck and Rachman's (1965) study, where classification is seen as fundamental to the scientific study of human personality. Eysenck and Rachman (1965) suggest that through the use of factor analysis, clustering groups of traits and then reducing these to super-ordinate measurements, individuals could be measured using standardised scales along two personality dimensions that could be shown to endure over time: extraversion-introversion and neuroticism-stability. Differences along these continuums were then said to be linked to biological differences. Eysenck and Rachman (1965) then contended that personality inventories could be used to make predictions about how people were likely to act in certain situations and make comparisons between individuals.

Interestingly, Eysenck and Rachman (1965) utilised the same four personality types as originally described by Hippocrates, yet clustered certain personality traits within these types, identified by psychometric questionnaires measuring personality across the two crossing continuums of introversion-extraversion and neurosis-stability. An interesting analogy can be made between extremes of these types and the characters of the Winnie-the-Pooh stories. The melancholic disposition (introverted-neurotic) exemplified by Eeyore's depressive nature (moody, rigid and pessimistic) and the social anxiety of Piglet (anxious, reserved and quiet). The choleric temperament (extraverted-neurotic) characterised by Tigger and possibly Roo (restless, excitable, impulsive, optimistic and active). There is also the phlegmatic characters (introverted-stable) of Owl and Pooh himself (passive, thoughtful, and calm), and even the sanguine personality (extraverted-stable) of Rabbit taken to the extreme of a somewhat authoritarian personality (outgoing, talkative and responsive). According to normative categorisations of abnormal deviance, all such extremes of psychiatric/ neurological divergence are pathologised with misguided attempts to normalise such character types. Even if this were possible, it is argued here that attempts at behavioural modification are like attempting to change the characters of the hundred-acre wood to be indistinguishable from Christopher Robin.

The same psychometric methodologies have been used in the creation of autism quotient tests (Baron-Cohen, 2003) and reflect an appeal to scientific credibility and an adherence to the use of quantitative data collection and analysis. In criticism to such approaches, Butt (2007) argues that social psychological knowledge, rather than being based on pre-existing phenomena waiting to be discovered, suggests that knowledge is constructed and situated historically and culturally. Knowledge, therefore, is seen as being socially situated and not a measurable and objective standard separated from those who produce it.

Trait theory rests upon the assumption that a consistent structure of personality resides in each individual person, yet perceptions of attributes related to others may have more to do with those doing the perceiving, than those being perceived. Traits from this view are nothing more than constructions in the eye of the beholder that reflect a world view of the perceiver, rooted within cultural ideologies and not a reflection of inner psychological dispositions of those being rated. Mischel (1968, cited in Butt, 2007) argues that attributions of disposition made about others reflect the perceptual prejudices of the onlooker. He found that people will rate others' attributes having observed them very briefly and that behavioural traits rarely show the consistency that trait theorists suggest. These findings suggest a fundamental attribution error is being made by trait theories, with those doing the rating attributing dispositions to the actions and behaviours of others without any justification. Mischel (1968, cited in Butt, 2007) also criticised the questionnaires used in psychometric testing, with words such as 'often' being construed to mean different things to different people and are thus an invalid indicator of some underlying trait. Accordingly, behaviour is theorised as much more context specific and situated. Thus, trait theory does not attempt to capture the unique richness of individual character, but rather measure and classify it.

It can be argued that the nomothetic approach adopted by trait theory offers little more than a description of behaviour and displays a circularity of reasoning, for example: explaining aggressive behaviour by saying someone is aggressive. In response to this criticism, such theorists suggest that personality traits can be related to underlying physiological factors. In so doing, they attempt to avoid the criticism that trait theory just re-describes phenomena, by positing a materialist account of behaviour and the mind-body problem within philosophy, an account for human action based in unchangeable and stable biological difference.

Within the framework of conditioned relativism, a diversity of dispositions ensues, yet rather than being unchangeable and stable differences based purely in biology, dispositions are also forged in unique social positionalities an ever-changing embodied sociality. In constant movement more analogous with the river flowing through the hundred-acre wood then the reductionist accounts of trait theorists.

'Nothing endures but change' (Heraclitus)

Social normativity and the sick role

'When you realise there is nothing lacking, the whole world belongs to you' (Lao Tzu)

In contrast to the philosophy of Hercalitus or Lao Tzu, alongside the ideology of normalcy, deviance and lack being symptomatic of psychological trait theorists through the ages, notions of social normativity have also flourished. Such normative theories have indeed dominated much political philosophy and early sociological theory, the founding fathers of normative sociological discourse being Auguste Comte and Emile Durkheim. Durkheim (1897) suggested that individuals had a personal need for a state of equilibrium regarding the regulation of one's moral values and integration into society. Too little or too much could lead to dysfunction and even suicide through social anomie. Thus people were seen to need a level of social control and sanction, for their own good and for the good of society. Despite Durkheim (1897) believing that society needed a certain amount of social deviance in order to maintain enough dynamism for change, he also argued that deviance was functional for reinforcing the norms and values of society. Thus the positioning of some of the population as deviant outsiders was an inevitable part of a functioning society, reifying inequality and notions of the idealised norm in contrast to a deviant other.

The functionalist notions of Durkheim (1897) were embedded within the sociological theorising of the Post-War American theorist Talcott Parsons (1951) who developed the theory of the sick role. Within this conceptualisation, illness and disability were seen as a deviancy from functional norms in need of professional monitoring and surveillance. Thus power became vested in the professional expert as a gatekeeper to the sick role and not the patient, literally seen as a role of being patient for the expert advice offered by the medical profession, which was to be followed in order to remediate one's condition and take one's place back in the economy. This system was seen as an ideal type model upon which to base service provision.

With rising life expectancy in many highly-developed societies in the post-war era, and increasing numbers of people being classified as long-term ill or disabled, Safilios-Rothschild (1970) expanded Parsonian notions of the sick role to include people who were deemed unable to achieve a level of functional norms: the rehabilitation role. The reasoning here consisting of those deemed disabled to make every effort to achieve as close a fit to normality as was possible, or as Goffman (1963) would have critiqued as leading to stigmatisation, to pass as normal.

Functionalist ideals of normalcy have dominated the field of autism studies, with the autistic lifeworld being invaded by a never-ending tide of interventions that try to eradicate autistic styles of diversity. Such a medicalisation and psychologisation of autism has led to internalised oppression and psycho-emotional disablement (Reeve, 2011; Milton & Lyte, 2012) and the rise in psychopharmacology in attempts to control and placate people with genuine problems of living.

'I cannot foresee Prozac gaining much more popularity, perhaps because of the stubbornness and perseverance of people like myself, who despite living through a "culture of depression", refuse to be swept along by the rise of psychopharmacology. At least that is, until the next "miracle drug" arrives, to enable us to live a more "normal" and "productive" life.' (Milton, 1999)

Fragmented phenomenological constructions of social reality

The phenomenologist Alfred Schutz (1967) split experiences of the social lifeworld into four different aspects: the umwelt (directly experienced social reality), mitwelt (experiences interacting with contemporaries), vorwelt (previous experiences) and fogwelt (imaginations of future possible experiences to come). For Schutz (1967), as people develop there is a general transition within the lifeworld between direct to indirect understandings of experience, leading to an increasing anonymity with what is directly experienced, whilst also creating and re-creating the experiencing of the world by themselves and others through their agency. Uexhull (1957) argued that an organism integrates experiences of the umwelt in what he termed the collective umwelt, somewhat similar to notions of the integration of central coherence in psychological theories of autism. Interestingly, Uexhull (1957) hypothesised that disruption to an organism could mean that such an integration would not operate efficiently.

It has been theorised by a number of autistic academics that autistic people can be somewhat characterised by a fragmented perception and experience of the social lifeworld as described by Alfred Schutz (1967). Murray *et al* (2005) suggest that autistic people have a tendency toward a monotropic focusing of perceptual interest and attention, yet this could be expressed in any number of different variations. Dawson (2012) argued that the cognitive domains within the brains of autistic people tend to work in relative isolation to one another. Pieper (1989) argued that it was the human capacity to reason which allowed them to live in welt (the social lifeworld), whilst plants and animals lived in an untamed umwelt. A lack of social reciprocity has often been cited as a deficit contained within the minds of autistic people (Baron-Cohen, 2003). Yet such theories psychologise what is essentially a socially negotiated interactive event. Indeed, the dispositions of autistic people are misunderstood themselves and ostracised for their otherness. The autistic experience of the lifeworld is often fragmented, but there also exists a double empathy problem between interacting agents of widely differing disposition and perception (Milton, 2012).

> *'He who knows, does not speak. He who speaks, does not know'*
> (Lao Tzu)

The metaphysical philosophy of Pirsig (1991) suggests a working model of dynamic and static quality to the properties of entities. As an example, language in this conceptualisation has a reified static quality of having been inscribed and exchanged. Dynamic quality, however, much more resembles the directly experienced umwelt as described by Schutz (1967). Autistic people could be said to exhibit a dynamic quality of perception, one less stratified by learnt schemas, one less socialised into obeying normative ideologies, but an embodied sociality nonetheless. Merleau-Ponty (1945) suggested that all consciousness was perceptual, with one's sense of the world and of oneself being an emergent property, an ongoing becoming. By seeing (autistic) people as uniquely and relativistically embodied, yet within an historical and social nexus, helps to dissolve the dogmatic distinctions of mind/body and individual/society.

Subverting the hegemony

'I'm gonna wave my freak flag high.' (Jimi Hendrix)

Despite various tensions between stakeholder groups, a dominant narrative persists in the field of autism studies that defines autism as a dysfunctional deviation from an idealised notion of normalcy, with little but tokenistic gestures being offered to autistic voices that are more often than not infantalised within debates. In subversion of this hegemony, however, have been the growth of autistic narratives and discourse, and the development of autistic culture and communities. In resisting the dominant ableism within the field, the notion of impairment and deficit and resultant normalisation agenda must be deconstructed. Autistic people will need to be utilising their voices in claiming ownership of the means of autistic production, and potentially celebrate the diversity of dispositions within and without the culture, or in the words of my great uncle:

'I wish no harm to any human being, but I, as one man, am going to exercise my freedom of speech. No human being on the face of the earth, no government is going to take from me my right to speak, my right to protest against wrong, my right to do everything that is for the benefit of mankind. I am not here, then, as the accused; I am here as the accuser of capitalism dripping with blood from head to foot.' (Maclean, 1919)

References

Baron-Cohen S (2003) *The Essential Difference*. London: Penguin.

Becker H (1963) *Outsiders*. New York: The Free Press.

Butt (2007) Individual differences. In: Langbridge D and Taylor S (eds). *Critical Readings in Social Psychology*. Milton Keynes: Open University.

Dawson M (2012) In conversation with... CRAE Seminar. Institute of Education.

Durkheim E (1897/1972) *Suicide*. London: Sage.

Eysenck H & Eysenck M (1958) *Personality and Individual Differences*. London: Plenum.

Eysenck H & Rachman S (1965) Dimensions of personality. In: Langbridge D and Taylor S (eds). *Critical Readings in Social Psychology*. Milton Keynes: Open University.

Hendrix J (1967) *If Six Was Nine*. Polydor Records.

Gell-Mann M (2002) *The Quark and the Jaguar: Adventures in the simple and the complex*. London: Owl Books.

Goffman E (1963) *Stigma: Notes on the management of a spoiled identity*. Harmondsworth: Penguin.

Maclean J (1919) *Speech from the Dock* [online]. Available at: www.marxists.org/archive/maclean/works/1918-dock.htm (accessed September 2017).

Marx K (1852) *The Eighteenth Brumaire of Louis Bonaparte*. In: R Tucker (ed) *The Marx-Engels Reader* (1970). New York: Norton, pp436–525.

Merleau-Ponty (1945) Phenomenology of Perception. London: Routledge.

Milton D (1999) *The Rise of Psychopharmacology* (unpublished). Masters essay: University of London.

Milton D (2012) On the ontological status of autism: the double empathy problem. *Disability and Society* **27** (6) 883–887.

Milton D & Lyte (2012) The normalisation agenda and the psycho-emotional disablement of autistic people. *Autonomy* **1** (1).

Murray D, Lesser M & Lawson W (2005) Attention, monotropism and the diagnostic criteria for autism. *Autism* **9** (2) 136–156.

Parsons T (1951) *The Social System*. New York: The Free Press.

Pieper J (1989) *An Anthology*. San-Francisco: Ignatius Press.

Pirsig R (1991) *Lila: An inquiry into morals*. London: Black Swan.

Reeve D (2011) Ableism within disability studies: The myth of the reliable and contained body. *Theorising Normalcy and the Mundane, 2nd International Conference*. Manchester Metropolitan University.

Safilios-Rothschild C (1970) The study of family power structure: a review 1960–1969. *Journal of Marriage and Family* **32** (4). Decade Review. Part 1 (Nov 1970): 539–552.

Schutz A (1967) *The Phenomenology of the Social World*. Evanston, IL: Northwestern University Press.

Autistic expertise: a critical reflection on the production of knowledge in autism studies

This essay is derived in part from an article published in Autism on 17 Mar 2014.

Abstract

The field of autism studies is a highly disputed territory within which competing contradictory discourses abound. In this field, it is the voices and claims of autistic people regarding their own expertise in knowledge production concerning autism that is most recent in the debate, and traditionally the least attended to. In this article, I utilise the theories of Harry Collins and colleagues in order to reflect upon and conceptualise the various claims to knowledge production and expertise within the field of autism studies, from the perspective of an author who has been diagnosed as being on the autism spectrum. The notion that autistic people lack sociality is problematised, with the suggestion that autistic people are not well described by notions such as the 'social brain', or as possessing 'zero degrees of cognitive empathy'. I then argue, however, that there is a qualitative difference in autistic sociality, and question to what extent such differences are of a biological or cultural nature, and to what extent interactional expertise can be gained by both parties in interactions between autistic and non-autistic people. In conclusion, I argue that autistic people have often become distrustful of researchers and their aims, and are frequently frozen out of the processes of knowledge production. Such a context results in a negative feedback spiral with further damage to the growth of interactional expertise between researchers and autistic people, and a breakdown in trust and communication leading to an increase in tension between stakeholder groups. The involvement of autistic scholars in research and improvements in participatory methods can thus be seen as a requirement, if social research in the field of autism is to claim ethical and epistemological integrity.

Introduction

Reflecting upon investigations carried out during doctoral research that concerned the discourses produced by various stakeholders regarding the education of autistic people, a range of views and opinions was being voiced by practitioners, academics from various disciplines, parents and autistic people themselves, and some clear trends have emerged (Milton, 2011; Milton, 2012c). These trends indicate a wide divide in outlook between the various personal deficit models of autism often favoured by practitioners and certain academics (Frith, 1989; Happe, 1994), and a more sociologically situated model of autism often followed by autistic people themselves (Arnold, 2010; Graby, 2012, Milton, 2012b).

The field of autism studies is a highly disputed territory with competing contradictory discourses abounding. Within this disputed territory, however, it has been the voice and assertion of autistic people themselves to claims of expertise in knowledge production that is most recent in the debate, and traditionally the least listened to (Milton & Bracher, 2013). This article utilises the theories of Harry Collins and his colleagues (Collins, 2004, 2010, 2011; Collins *et al*, 2006; Collins & Evans, 2007) in order to reflect upon and conceptualise the various claims to knowledge production and expertise within the field of autism studies.

The article proceeds in six sections. The section called 'A framework to conceptualise expertise' outlines the framework for conceptualising the acquisition of knowledge and expertise by Collins and Evans (2007). This section then introduces the term of 'interactional expertise' and asks to what extent such mutual understanding is achievable between autistic and non-autistic people. This framework was originally devised to indicate that the kind of expertise employed by specialists is often of a socially situated nature. The section 'Popular understandings' (p63) shows how such a framework can account for some of the popular understandings (and misunderstandings) that can be seen in the field of autism for those who do not have access to such specialist practices. In the section 'The 'machine-like' metaphor' (p64), the 'machine-like' metaphor often used to describe autistic cognition and knowledge acquisition is critiqued utilising this conceptual framework, and an argument put forward that autistic people (across the spectrum) are indeed social beings, albeit perhaps a more idiosyncratic or outsider social experience and expressions of social agency. This argument is continued in the section 'Autism and the acquisition of tacit knowledge' (p66), which explores in depth the ways in which knowledge can be acquired, and how autistic people cannot be said to totally lack such forms of knowledge. This section finishes with a critique of educational methods for autistic people that break down social information into explicit 'rules'. The section 'How does one know when interactional expertise with autistic culture has been acquired?' (p68) asks the important question of how one is to know when one has gained interactional expertise with autistic people and their culture, seen by Collins and Evans (2007) as a minimal requirement for social scientific research on cultural groups. This section reviews the use of the 'imitation game' as devised by Collins and Evans (2007), an adaptation of the Turing Test, where the 'judge' has to decide between two people, one who is a genuine member of a cultural group and one who is an imposter. If such a game were to be played by social researchers in the field of autism studies, it would give an indication as to the level of interactional expertise gained, and whether interpretations by said researcher are likely to be relevant and accurate. The section 'Lost in translation?' (p70) asks whether or not due to embodied differences between autistic and nonautistic people, whether some level of understanding will always be 'lost in translation', and whether the 'double empathy problem' (Milton, 2012b) can be reduced and to what extent. The article finishes with some final remarks regarding the need for the involvement of autistic scholars in social research regarding autistic people, the increased use of participatory methods, and sets a challenge for social researchers working in this field.

A framework to conceptualise expertise

In recent decades, scholars in social theory have developed increasingly more sophisticated accounts of the nature of scientific expertise. This work explains how different claims to knowledge are defended by reference to different sorts of specialism or expertise. Collins and Evans (2007) in *Rethinking Expertise* set out a 'periodic table of expertise' based on the notion of socially located domains of tacit knowledge, that is, knowledge that cannot easily be made explicit or codified. This framework being predicated on a conceptual working model of loose boundaries between the categories stated. This conceptualisation was taken further in *Tacit and Explicit Knowledge*, in which Collins (2010) provides a conceptual language with which to analyse the acquisition of knowledge.

Collins and Evans (2007) suggest that expertise is primarily based on the acquisition of tacit knowledge. In theorising tacit knowledge, they distinguish between ubiquitous and specialist expertise. Ubiquitous expertise includes an endless number of skills and knowledge that sustain the forms of life and culture of society (e.g. fluency in natural language or moral sensibility), whereas specialist expertise requires immersion in the language and practice of expert communities. Collins and Evans (2007) rank the acquisition of specialist knowledge on a scale of expertise running from 'beer-mat knowledge', through 'popular understanding', and 'primary source knowledge', all being knowledge which can be acquired from a base of ubiquitous tacit knowledge, before attaining 'interactional' and finally 'contributory' expertise, which depend on the acquisition of specialist tacit knowledge.

The differences between these categories of expertise are subtle, however, and relate to the availability of socialisation into practice communities. Specialist expertise can therefore be seen as a socially restricted form of socialisation (i.e. cultural learning dependent on being embedded in a specialist social practice), while the other forms of ubiquitous expertise are said to be available to all. When one applies such categorisations to the knowledge and expertise displayed by autistic people, things tend to look a bit different. Specialist expertise can certainly be found, not least with autistic culture, community and language (Arnold, 2010; Lawson, 2008; Sinclair, 1993; 1999), yet more common forms of ubiquitous expertise are often deemed to be deficient or lacking due to cognitive deficit, such as the ability for 'dynamic thinking' (Gustein, 2000), or 'cognitive empathy' (Baron-Cohen, 2012).

Following Wittgenstein, Collins and Evans (2007) argue that it is in the use of a concept which determines its meaning, thus understanding specialist meaning takes immersion in a way of life, rather than information gathering alone. In acquiring initial 'beer-mat' knowledge or simple popular understandings, such deep immersion is not required, and as such the specialist ubiquitous expertise of 'ordinary people' should not be confused with the expertise of technical specialists within a particular domain of knowledge. The amount of interactional expertise achievable between autistic and non-autistic people, or how much these barriers are cultural, biological or whether such a distinction can be made (Hacking, 2009) has not been adequately 'answered' or investigated through a sociological or contextualised lens in sufficient depth. As will be returned to later in this article, however, I argue that some level of interactional expertise must be possible, as no autistic person is completely uncommunicative. The interactional expertise shown by non-autistic social researchers is, however, often clearly insufficient, given the criticisms made of such investigations by autistic scholars (Arnold, 2012a; Milton & Bracher, 2013). Gaining expertise in what it is to be autistic would take immersion in the culture and practices of autistic people, yet it is questionable as to what extent such immersion is possible for non-autistic people and it is certainly doubtful that many established scientists have made the effort. Yet, for Collins and Evans (2007), interactional expertise should be seen as a basic standard for social scientific research. Such a gap in understanding can be seen as adding to the distrust and offence taken by autistic people to how 'we' as a group are examined, inspected and interpreted by those of a non-autistic dispositionality; as Moon, a neurodiverse activist has stated, being 'fishbowled' (Milton & Moon, 2012a). It should also be remembered who the 'contributory experts' are, regarding the creation of autistic subjectivity and culture in the first place: autistic people themselves. Interactive expertise does not make someone an autistic person contributing to autistic culture, but someone more able to engage and interact with autistic language and communications. The involvement of autistic scholars in research and improvements in participatory methods can thus be seen as a requirement, if social research in the field of autism is to claim ethical and epistemological integrity.

Claims to knowledge are of course linked to power and social closure (the restricting and privileging of social opportunities for one group of people at the expense of another) which influence the social valuing of various forms of specialist expertise (Rose, 1999). It is sometimes suggested in the case of autistic people, moreover, that an apparent inability to acquire basic forms of ubiquitous expertise lead autistic people to be unable to develop specialist expertise, even with reference to their own subjectivity and social positionality (e.g. Hendriks, 2012). Instead, expertise that is remarked upon as being achievable by some autistic people is seen in much non-autistic literature on the subject as residing in some kind of exotic other, within a discourse of the extraordinary autistic 'savant' (Arnold, 2012b). Such a lack of social expertise and understanding has been called into question, however, by the initial emergence of autistic autobiographies, followed by autistic scholarship and the rise of advocacy organisations run by autistic people themselves (such as the Autistic Rights Group Highland (ARGH), Autonomy or Autscape). It is of course true that not all autistic people are capable of such expressiveness, but a number of autistic people thought to have been incapable of communicating have found ways in which to do so (Wurzberg, 2011).

Popular understandings

Due to the specialised nature of expertise, Collins and Evans (2007) suggest that scientists must simplify their work in order to explain something of it to a professional audience, and even more for popular audiences:

'…in the case of disputed science, a level of understanding equivalent to popular understanding is likely to yield poor technical judgements.' (Collins & Evans, 2007: 21)

Popular understandings can lead to polarised reactions to scientific research. This can sometimes involve accepting a simplified version of evidence as truth and fact. We see this, for example, in the way that the idea of there being a theory of mind deficit in autism is now commonly depicted as 'factual' in popular literature, despite it being more accurately described as a working model or partial heuristic in the scientific world. Or it can involve the acceptance of claims without due thought. This is witnessed in the promotion of false conspiracy theories, as in the moral panic regarding vaccines and autism. For Collins and Evans (2007), such misinterpretations are strengthened by media representations of disputed science as something more revealing of knowledge being produced within a community of experts. One could also say, however, that popular misunderstandings are exacerbated by the claims of some academics themselves. The use of crude terms such as an 'extreme male brain' with reference to autism in the scientific literature could clearly help produce unsurprisingly simplistic understandings outside the scientific community (Baron-Cohen, 2008).

The 'machine-like' metaphor

The tendency discussed earlier for the scientific community to neglect the specific expertise of the autistic community is further exacerbated by the widely prevailing notion that autistic people are somehow 'machine-like' or lacking in the socialisation necessary for effective communication. Asperger (1991) himself wrote that:

'The autist is only himself … and is not an active member of a greater organism which he is influenced by and which he influences constantly.' (Asperger, 1991: 38)

Approaches to the ontology of autism have been evolving ever since the phenomenon came into the clinical lexicon, yet the notion of the autistic person somehow being 'machine-like', incapable of true socialisation, possessing 'zero degrees of empathy' or having an impairment in their 'social brain' (Baron-Cohen, 2012), has remained a repeated descriptive metaphor (Hendriks, 2012).

Collins (2010) utilises the notion of strings as building blocks of signs and symbols, a physical object that only has an effect due to what happens to it. While language is conceptualised as a set of meanings located in society, strings are conceptualised as base objects that are the means by which language is inscribed and shared. Collins (2010) suggests that computers deal in strings and not language interpretation. No string has inherent meaning, as it is in linguistic interpretation that meaning is constructed and negotiated. Autistic people are often misinterpreted as only being able to deal in strings of information, as though they totally lacked a sociality and a language, or as though lacking meaning-making emotions.

A recent example of this phenomenon is seen within the theory and practice of Relationship Development Intervention (Gustein, 2000), where autistic people are depicted as lacking 'dynamic thinking' and possessing instead a strength in 'static thinking' (in other words, processing strings of information). Yet, autistic artwork (Mullin, 2009) or the 'non-verbal' language expressed by

Amanda Baggs (2007) is not reducible to strings alone in terms of how they are produced, but an engagement with the collective lifeworld of social life (i.e. learnt through some kind of sharing of social experiences).

The implications of this prevailing misunderstanding of autistic socialisation are extensive. Collins and Evans (2007) suggest that there has been a general move towards seeing knowledge and ability as concerning embodied experience or else competence, that is, what one 'does' is what matters rather than just what someone can 'reproduce' (cited in Collins & Evans, 2007). For Collins and Evans (2007), moreover, the primary site of the acquisition of knowledge and expertise is social, thus the mastering of a skill requires more than the embodiment of it, but the socialisation of people into relevant social practices. This, they say, is the difference between being able simply physically to balance on a bike and actually being able to negotiate traffic. Collins and Evans (2007) argue that polymorphic actions (actions that depend on context for interpretation and continuation and thus not reproducible by machines) require social understanding and flexibility to adapt actions to changing social contexts. This is the reason given by Collins and Evans (2007) to suggest why machines cannot replicate humans. If one is to believe current dominant ideologies regarding what autism is, then, it could also be argued that autistic people are machine-like, and unable to replicate appropriately the behaviours and understandings of non-disordered humans (at least without 'intervention'). There is clearly a need to correct this ideological error. Although processing of strings of information can be a strength found among many on the autism spectrum (Murray *et al*, 2005), not all autistic displays of knowledge and expertise can be explained away as highly honed mimeomorphic actions (actions performed in the same way each time and thus can be reproduced mechanically). With autistic people, especially those who acquire verbal articulacy, one often finds the sociality of an 'outsider' (Becker, 1963), an alienated social identity, but a social identity nonetheless. Also, it is often said that one of the most defining features of autism is a 'spiky' cognitive profile (Milton, 2012c) that can lead to extreme strengths in areas of mimeomorphic actions, but also potentially a widening of perspective and a distinctive kind of sociality, particularly in later years of development. Such a sociality is often stigmatised (Milton, 2013b) rather than being seen as a potential asset within communities of practice.

Autism and the acquisition of tacit knowledge

What the argument so far demonstrates is that it is necessary to develop a clear account of the kinds of knowledge that autistic people may be able to acquire and to reject misplaced assumptions which prevent us from doing just that. In his conception of the acquisition of tacit knowledge, Collins (2010) demarcates three main categories: weak/relational, medium/somatic and strong/collective. Weak relational tacit knowledge arises from social interaction, yet any piece of it in principle can be made explicit. Collins (2010) gives the example of an experienced warehouseman who can find specific objects within a warehouse, yet would not be able to list every object; however, one could program a computer to do just this task. At times, knowledge that can be made explicit is not due to accident, lack of time or, as Collins (2010) indicates, 'mismatched saliences'.

For Collins (2010), somatic tacit knowledge is knowledge that can be explained or written down but cannot be used in a pragmatic way by humans due to the limitations of their bodies (their 'somatic affordances'). Such knowledge can in principle be made explicit, yet may be very difficult to do so. Machines of the right design may be able to apply such knowledge due to differing somatic affordance (e.g. machines can compute mathematical sums far quicker than humans can). Somatic-affordance tacit knowledge can only be performed and applied as actions in practice due to the affordances of the materials from which a body or entity is made. In this respect, the limit is not explicability but embodiment. Strong or collective tacit knowledge, as defined by Collins (2010), can only be acquired through immersion in the language and practices of society and is conceptualised as a property of society. In this conceptualisation, individuals are seen as 'parasitic' on the body of social knowledge (or needing to draw upon social experiences to form tacit knowledge). This ability to be 'parasitic' on the social body is a unique property of humans, as neither other animals nor

A Mismatch of Salience: Explorations of the nature of autism from theory to practice
© Pavilion Publishing and Media Ltd and its licensors 2017.

machines are capable of such collective knowledge acquisition. The term used by Collins (2010) to identify this split is 'social Cartesianism'.

An interesting example utilised by Collins (2010) is the description of a scene from *Star Trek: The Next Generation* regarding the character of Lt Commander Data, a character often described as being representative of an autistic persona. In the scene, Data was able to learn dance steps to a routine without difficulty, and then in time was able to improvise dance steps of his own. Collins (2010) rightly points out that a machine would not be capable of improvisation. Yet, as an example, if I were to be placed in such a situation, it would be virtually impossible for me to enact a set dance routine, but I would have no trouble at all in improvising one, whether such a dance would win any awards in the eyes of others is debatable though. Collins (2010) points out that domesticated animals, while immersed in human society, are not able to be socialised, in the sense one does not encounter vegetarian, arty or nerdy dogs, they are simply just dogs. This sociality is often said to be impaired in autistic people, even mentioned by Collins (2011) when using as an example of the autistic savant who appears to manage their performances in the absence of collective tacit knowledge, with this absence seeming to be a principal feature of the autistic lifeworld. Yet, one does encounter autistic people who are vegetarian, artistic and certainly nerdy. Autistic people have distinct interests and abilities that involve social practices, and this includes those who are deemed 'non-verbal', who are often musical or artistic and whose bodily movements have been argued to be a form of language (Baggs, 2007; Milton, 2013a).

If autistic people are primarily machine-like, then where do the idiosyncratic expressions of autistic people (Mullin, 2009) originate? If one were to follow the theory of Murray *et al* (2005), perhaps it is the affordances of an autistic mind-set leading to the honing-in on particular aspects of the social which inspire interest and attention – a monotropic social being, with a fragmented experience of the social. Indeed, if artificial intelligence is one day produced, it may perform similarly to an autistic person, but this performance may contain a liking for unusual improvisation:

> *'What is being argued is that humans differ from animals, trees, and sieves in having a unique capacity to absorb social rules from the surrounding society – rules that change from place to place, circumstance to circumstance, and time to time.'* (Collins, 2010: 124)

Autistic people are often taught social 'rules' as if they are more fixed and static than they actually are in lived reality, which only causes more confusion. Much social skill or behavioural training with autistic people is predicated upon breaking down such information into explicated strings of information, which does little to help autistic people adjust to the changing flux of negotiated socially constructed realities (Milton, 2012b). By the use of such methods, autistic people have their fragmented social perceptions reinforced via the very way 'social skills' are being taught. Recently, however, methods such as Intensive Interaction (Nind & Hewitt, 1994), which focus on relationship building and child-led activities, have begun to challenge this dominance within the field.

How does one know when interactional expertise with autistic culture has been acquired?

Following the argument presented here, one of the primary tasks facing those attempting to work with autistic people or to analyse the nature of autism is to appreciate the distinctive knowledge autistic people possess, and to build more constructive ways of relating to it. As Hacking (2009) puts it:

> *'They are creating the language in which to describe the experience of autism, and hence helping to forge the concepts in which to think autism.'* (Hacking, 2009: 1467)

Over the past two decades, there has been the growth of a variety of autistic communities, both online and in conferences run by and for autistic people, such as Autscape (2013). Following the insights of Collins and Evans (2007), in order to study such a social group, interactional expertise is needed. The amount of interactional expertise and understanding of autistic culture exhibited by social researchers in the field, however, has often left a great deal to be desired (Arnold, 2012a). Misrepresentations of autistic culture are widespread within current literature and have hampered progress in the field (Milton & Bracher, 2013). When autistic people have been involved in research, this has often added much to the work produced, as the recent work of the Autism Education Trust demonstrates (Wittemeyer *et al*, 2011; Wittemeyer *et al*, 2012).

Collins (2004) argues that interactional expertise can simply be seen in the ways an individual can interact within a practice community, and that it is a quality utilised by specialist journalists and championed by interpretive social scientific methods (Collins *et al*, 2006), a form of realist pragmatic 'verstehen' (an understanding of the intentions and motives behind the actions of others). In order to test the level of interactional expertise one has with an outsider group to one's own, Collins *et al* (2006) devised an alternative to the Turing test, known as the 'imitation game'. Collins *et al* (2006) suggested that imitation games investigate the specific linguistic abilities of interactional experts, contributory experts and non-experts. These experiments utilise three computers linked via a wireless network with specialist software. Judges who are contributory experts type questions to the other participants, probing for possession of expertise. One participant is genuine and the other is someone without contributory expertise. After each question, the judge makes a guess with a confidence level associated with the guess. The session continues until the judge feels there is nothing left to be gained by continuing. Interactional expertise is purported to be demonstrated whenever the proportion of correct guesses is greater than that which would have been achieved by chance alone. The confidence levels of guesses are split into the following four levels:

Level 1: I have little or no idea who is who.
Level 2: I have some idea who is who – but I am more unsure than I am sure.
Level 3: I have a good idea who is who – and I am more sure than unsure.
Level 4: I am pretty sure I know who is who.

Guesses at level 3 or 4 of confidence are scored as either correct or incorrect, while all guesses right or wrong at levels 1 and 2 are counted as being uncertain. Whenever judges change their level of confidence, they are asked as to why this is the case. A second phase to the test is then to send the dialogues contained to a set of more judges.

Imitation game experiments conducted by Collins *et al* (2006) show that those well socialised into the language of a specialist group are linguistically indistinguishable from those with full practical socialisation, yet distinguishable from those who are not well socialised into such specialised discourses. Thus, tacit knowledge of specialist languages can be acquired without having the tacit knowledge associated with the practices of specialist cultures to the level of contributory expertise.

If one were to apply the methodology of imitation games within the field of autism studies, a number of issues would need to be taken into account, such as general linguistic ability, potential personal connections between judge and participant, asking autistic people to potentially lie and so on. Having said this, they would no doubt yield interesting results. Would academics, practitioners and even parents be able to pass such a test in pretending to be autistic? Would social theorists who write about the autistic community and the neurodiversity movement be able to pass as a self-advocate? Such a test would give some indication as to the level of interactional expertise gained, and whether interpretations of autistic communities and culture can be said to be relevant and accurate depictions.

Lost in translation?

Interactional expertise can be seen as an important step towards mutual understanding, yet in the case of interactions between autistic and non-autistic people, is something always going to be 'lost in translation'? When differences in disposition and social understandings have foundations in neurological diversity, how much interactional expertise is possible? Is some level of expertise in what it is to be autistic on a phenomenological level of lived experience always beyond the grasp of non-autistic social scientific researchers? It could be said that autism is a state-specific expertise (Collins & Evans, 2007). Is the somatic affordance (the limitations of one's physiology) of an autistic bodily state a necessary condition for interactional expertise regarding autistic subjectivity? If this is the case, then interactional expertise between autistic and non-autistic people would always be constrained and partial at best. Both the philosophers Nagel (1974/1981) and Wittgenstein (cited in Collins & Evans, 2007) wrote thought experiments regarding the possibility of understanding what it would be like to be an animal (other than human). Nagel asked the question 'What is it like to be a Bat?', while Wittgenstein asked the question, 'If a Lion could speak, would a human being be able to understand it?'. The conclusions of these thought experiments were that it was impossible to conceptualise of such an 'other', and to remove oneself from one's own perceptions and somatic (embodied) limitations. So, if the somatic affordances of autistic and non-autistic people are significantly different, is understanding the autistic lifeworld in the perceptions of a non-autistic onlooker a more nuanced version of understanding the perception of a bat or attempting to speak 'Lionese' (and vice versa)? This difficulty is exacerbated by what might be called the 'double empathy problem' (Milton, 2012b). Collins (2004) wrote that:

> 'Certainly, almost everything I write, and that includes the straightforward pieces, seems open to astonishing misinterpretation by at least a few people.' (Collins, 2004: 105)

While Collins (2004) was referring to the way in which his own writings are misinterpreted, such a breakdown in communication is a daily experience for autistic people (Milton 2013b). The autistic form of life does not conform to assumed social normativity and does not easily extend outward into the social, leading to a 'double empathy problem' between people of diverse dispositions (Milton, 2012b), that is, both parties struggle to understand and relate to one another. Such differences in presentation can lead to dyspathic reactions (Cameron, 2012) and stigma (Milton, 2013b), often leading to ill-fated attempts at normalisation and a continuing vicious cycle of psycho-emotional disablement (Milton & Moon, 2012b).

Collins and Evans (2007) put forward a minimal embodiment thesis and social embodiment thesis to the acquisition of knowledge. Yet, when brains do operate differently and affect social embodiment, a double empathy problem ensues easily. Reaching interactional expertise may be blocked by embodied differences of somatic affordance. Yet, for all the language and rhetoric of being from a 'different planet' or feeling like an 'anthropologist on mars', autistic people remain both human and social, albeit idiosyncratically, with diverse experiences of socialisation, or the lack of access into communities of practice to be immersed in. Such a lack of access to communities of practice can also lead to social isolation and anomie and negative consequences for individual mental and physical well-being (Milton & Moon, 2012b). Indeed, the construction of another 'silo' (linguistic community of experts) of the neurodiversity movement can be seen as an attempt to break down the 'silo mentality' itself (Arnold, 2010; Milton, 2012d) within the study of autism. Thankfully, there are now the beginnings of a more concerted effort from researchers, both autistic and nonautistic, to improve the participatory nature of the research agenda (Milton *et al*, 2012; Milton & Bracher, 2013; Pellicano, 2012; Pellicano *et al*, 2013). Yet, difficulties remain even if the effort is made.

In the field of autism studies, little produces more debate than claims as to 'who can speak for autistic people' (Pellicano, 2012; Rudavsky, 2011). All stakeholder groups make differing claims to specialist contributory knowledge, but working within differing communities of practice with differing frames of reference. One could speculate that the sociological awareness of many neuroscientists studying autism could fail at the 'beer-mat' challenge, and vice versa, given the ever-increasing specialism inherent in academic training. As Collins put it:

'Developmental psychology offers valuable insights into the processes humans go through as they become parasites on collective tacit knowledge but the explanation is far from complete.'
(Collins, 2010: 145)

The mutual incomprehension that Collins (2011) talks about as a potential consequence of the lack of the centrality of language and humans as 'social parasites' is exactly what often happens in interactions between autistic and non-autistic people, even when verbal skills have been gained. In order to build bridges and practice languages, at the very least, autistic people need to be listened to (Milton *et al*, 2012; Milton & Bracher, 2013; Pellicano, 2012; Pellicano *et al*, 2013):

> *'Indeed, it is hard to see why mutual incomprehension would not go right down to the level of individual personal experience.'*
> (Collins, 2011: 283)

Final remarks

According to the minimal embodiment thesis of Collins and Evans (2007) regarding interactional expertise, people who cannot perform a particular task or skill, and who therefore cannot have the embodied expertise associated with it, can still talk about that skill as if they did possess the embodied skills. Interactional expertise thus raises a key question about the level of embodiment that is needed for expertise to be transferred. For proponents of the embodiment thesis, quite a lot of embodiment is required, yet from the perspective of Collins and Evans (2007), much less embodiment is generally needed:

> *'The claim associated with the idea of interactional expertise is that mastery of an entire form of life is not necessary for the mastery of the language pertaining to the form of life. This is a big claim and needs strong proof.'* (Collins & Evans, 2007: 77)

The somatic affordance of autistic and non-autistic dispositions may well create a large double empathy problem (Milton, 2012b), where both have a difficulty in understanding the nuances of one another's perception and sociality. To what extent can anyone immerse themselves in the language and culture of the other? At least some must be the answer, as autistic people are not 'aliens' despite the popular use of the term within autistic culture. Such an immersion can also be said to be the inspiration of approaches to the education of autistic people that have a more child-led focus (Milton, 2012c):

> *'The position argued here is that you do not have to use your body (acquire contributory expertise) in order to speak the language of the domain (acquire interactional expertise)…'* (Collins & Evans, 2007: 78)

This is a debatable position, however, if one considers autistic language can be 'non-verbal' and based upon bodily movements and sensations (Baggs, 2007; Milton, 2012a). In my view, the level of embodiment needed for interactional expertise with autistic people remains unanswered, yet the imitation game experiments devised by Collins and Evans (2007) may provide a starting point by which this topic could be explored further.

It must also be remembered who, in this conceptualisation, are the contributory experts regarding autistic subjectivity and culture, for this does take embodiment – that is, autistic people themselves.

In the history of autism studies, expertise has been claimed by many differing academic schools of thought, practitioners, parents, quacks and so on. Yet, the one voice that has been traditionally silenced within the field is that of autistic people themselves. Due to a lack of interactional expertise with autistic communities (Arnold, 2012b; Milton & Bracher, 2013), one could say a negative spiral has ensued. Consequently, autistic people have often become distrustful of researchers and their aims and are frozen out of processes of knowledge production (Milton *et al*, 2012). Such a context results in a lack of interactional expertise between researchers and autistic people and a breakdown in trust and communication (Milton, 2012b) leading to an increase in tension between stakeholder groups (Milton, 2011).

Finally, it is hoped that those wanting to research the sociality of autistic people may take up the challenge of an imitation game.

Acknowledgements

The author would like to thank Harry Collins, Rob Evans and Mike Bracher for their commentary during the development of this article.

Funding

This research received no specific grant from any funding agency in the public, commercial or not-for-profit sectors.

References

Arnold L (2010) The medium is the message [online]. Available at: www.ucl.ac.uk/cpjh/Arnold (accessed 16 February 2012).

Arnold L (2012a) Autism (book review). *Disability and Society* **27** (5) 729–730.

Arnold L (2012b) The social construction of the savant. In: *Critical disability studies conference*, Lancaster University, Lancaster.

Asperger H (1991/1944) Autistic psychopathy in childhood. In: Frith U (ed.) *Autism and Asperger syndrome*. Cambridge University Press, pp.37–92.

Baggs A (2007) In my language [online]. Available at http://www.youtube.com/watch?v=JnylM1hI2jc (accessed October 2017).

Baron-Cohen S (2008) *Autism and Asperger Syndrome (The Facts)*. Oxford: Oxford University Press.

Baron-Cohen S (2012) *Zero Degrees of Empathy: A new understanding of cruelty and kindness*. Harmondsworth: Pensguin Books.

Becker H (1963) *Outsiders*. New York: Free Press.

Cameron L (2012) *Dyspathy: The dynamic complement of empathy*. Milton Keynes: The Open University.

Collins H (2004) How do you know you've alternated? *Social Studies of Science* **34** 103–106.

Collins H (2010) *Tacit and Explicit Knowledge*. London: University of Chicago Press.

Collins H (2011) Language and practice. *Social Studies of Science* **41** (2) 271–300.

Collins H & Evans R (2007) *Rethinking Expertise*. London: University of Chicago Press.

Collins H, Evans R, Ribeiro R & Hall M (2006) Experiments with interactional expertise. *Studies in History and Philosophy of Science* 37 656–674.

Frith U (1989) *Autism: Explaining the enigma.* London: Wiley-Blackwell.

Graby S (2012) To be or not to be disabled: autism, disablement and identity politics. Paper presented at the *Theorising Normalcy and the Mundane* conference, University of Chester, Chester, 27 June.

Gustein S (2000) *Autism Aspergers: Solving the relationship puzzle – a new developmental program that opens the door to lifelong social and emotional growth*. Arlington, TX: Future Horizons.

Hacking I (2009) Autistic autobiography. *Philosophical Transactions of the Royal Society B: Biological Sciences* **364** (1522) 1467–1473.

Happe F (1994) *Autism: An introduction to psychological theory.* London: Psychology Press.

Hendriks R (2012) *Autistic Company*. Amsterdam: Rodopi Bv Editions.

Lawson W (2008) *Concepts of Normality: The autistic and typical spectrum.* London: Jessica Kingsley.

Milton D (2011) Educational discourse and the autistic student: an 'inside-out' approach. In: *9th annual postgraduate education conference*, University of Birmingham, Birmingham, 5 July 2010.

Milton D (2012a) Embodied sociality and the conditioned relativism of dispositional diversity. In: *Theorising Normalcy 2012*, University of Chester, Chester, 26 June.

Milton D (2012b) On the ontological status of autism: the double empathy problem. *Disability and Society* **27** (6) 883–887.

Milton D (2012c) *So What Exactly Is Autism?* London: Autism Education Trust.

Milton D (2012d) Theorising autism. In: *Theorising autism pilot day*, University of Birmingham, Birmingham, 28 September.

Milton D (2013a) Clumps: and autistic reterritorialisation of the rhizome. In: *Theorising normalcy and the mundane. 4th International Conference*, Sheffield Hallam University, 4 September 2013.

Milton D (2013b) 'Filling in the gaps', a micro-sociological analysis of autism. *Autonomy* **1** (2).

Milton D & Bracher M (2013) Autistics speak but are they heard? *Medical Sociology Online* **7** (2) 61–69.

Milton D & Moon L (2012a) 'And that Damian is what I call life changing': findings from an action research project involving autistic adults in an online sociology study group. *Good Autism Practice* **13** (2) 32–39.

Milton D & Moon L (2012b) The normalisation agenda and the psycho-emotional disablement of autistic people. *Autonomy, the Critical Journal of Interdisciplinary Autism Studies* **1** (1).

Milton D, Mills R & Pellicano L (2012) Ethics and autism: where is the autistic voice? Commentary on Post *et al. Journal of Autism and Developmental Disorders*. DOI: 10.1007/s10803-012-1739-x.

Mullin J (2009) *Drawing Autism*. New York: Mark Batty.

Murray D, Lesser M & Lawson W (2005) Attention, monotropism and the diagnostic criteria for autism. *Autism* **9** (2) 136–156.

Nagel T (1974/1981) What is it like to be a bat? In: DR Hofstadter and DC Dennett (eds) *The Mind's I: Fantasies and reflections on self and soul*. London: Penguin Books, pp391–402.

Nind M & Hewitt D (1994) *Access to Communication*. London: David Fulton.

Pellicano L (2012) *Who Should Speak for Autistic People?* London: Institute of Education.

Pellicano L, Dinsmore A & Charman T (2013) *A Future Shaped Together: Shaping autism research in the UK*. London: Institute of Education.

Rose N (1999) *Governing the Soul: Shaping of the private self.* London: Free Press.

Rudavsky S (2011) *Adults with autism speak out* [online]. USA Today. Available at: http://usatoday30.usatoday.com/news/nation/story/2011-11-06/autism-adults/51089566/1 (accessed September 2017).

Sinclair J (1993) *Don't Mourn for Us* [online]. Available at: http://www.autreat.com/dont_mourn.html (accessed September 2017).

Sinclair J (1999) *Why I Dislike 'Person-First' Language* [online]. Deleted from: http://www.cafemom.com/journals/read/436505/.

Wittemeyer K, Charman T, Cusack J *et al* (2011) *Educational Provision and Outcomes for People on the Autism Spectrum*. London: Autism Education Trust.

Wittemeyer K, English A, Jones G *et al* (2012) *The Autism Education Trust Professional Competency Framework*. London: Autism Education Trust.

Wurzberg G (2011) *Wretches & Jabberers*. State of the Art, Inc. Available at: http://www.wretchesandjabberers.org/ (accessed September 2017).

Part three:
From theory to practice

The third section of this collection moves beyond theory to how the concepts explored so far can impact on practice and the lived experience of autistic people. This section contains four chapters, beginning with an essay exploring the potential for utilising micro-sociological theory and research practice, and advancing the notion that autistic people may struggle to 'fill in the gaps' in social understanding based upon previously constructed schemas. The second chapter in this section analyses the diversity of views that exist and tensions between the various interventions promoted to be used with autistic children. The third chapter in this section is a reflection on the 'non-interventionist' work of Fernand Deligny, an unconventional philosopher and practitioner who worked with non-verbal autistic people in communes that he set up, following anything but a normalising agenda. The final chapter in this section was originally produced in support of the '7 days of action' campaign. This essay applies seven sociological concepts to the dehumanising treatment so often metered out to autistic people with significant learning disabilities.

Filling in the gaps: a micro-sociological analysis of autism

This article was first published in the Autonomy journal in 2013, having been presented initially at the Theorising Normalcy and the Mundane conference in 2011.

Abstract

When reviewing research related to autism, it is clear that it is dominated by biological and psychological concerns, with autism being defined as a developmental deviance, dysfunction and deficit. Much of this research assumes a functionalist philosophy regarding deviations from statistical norms as pathological and in need of remediation. This research feeds into a hegemonic view of what constitutes normalcy, with critical social explanations being lost under the sheer mass of research from this viewpoint. Despite the ascendency of this functionalist philosophy, there is a growing concern regarding listening to autistic voices from a phenomenological perspective (Biklen, 2005) and with regards to the wider social construction of autism (Nadesan, 2005; Timini *et al*, 2011). However, the study of autism on a micro-sociological level has been given precious little attention. This paper utilises the theories of Garfinkel (1967) and Goffman (1955; 1959; 1963; 1974) in particular, in order to question current ways of perceiving autism, highlighting issues concerning social interactions involving autistic people, and the stigma of autism, as well as deconstructing the myth of a lack of empathy (Baron-Cohen, 2008; 2011).

Introduction

A currently popular model for researching health issues is the biopsychosocial (BPS) model of health (Engel, 1977). This model attempts to move beyond the traditional biomedical model of health that framed health and illness in terms of a biological deviation from normal functioning, due to pathogens, developmental abnormalities, or injury. The BPS model looks beyond this reductionist framework to include psychological and social factors that affect health, with each factor interacting and impacting on each other. The model has been criticised however, for a lack of theoretical integration between these factors, and for simply stating an obvious fact (Pilgrim, 2002). Pilgrim (2002) also states that the BPS model has not been fully realised and that the biomedical model is still dominant.

When reviewing research related to autism, it is clear that it is dominated by biological and psychological concerns, with autism being defined as a developmental deviance, dysfunction and deficit. Much of this research assumes a functionalist philosophy regarding deviations from statistical norms as pathological, and in need of remediation. This philosophy is taken for granted when looking at the social context of autism, in which autistic people are perceived to be socially abnormal and dysfunctional, with much policy related research taking an economic perspective of the cost of autism (Knapp *et al*, 2009). This research feeds into a hegemonic view of what constitutes normalcy, with critical social explanations being lost under the sheer mass of research from this viewpoint.

> *'Although there is a biological aspect to this condition named autism, the social factors involved in its identification, representation, interpretation, remediation, and performance are the most important factors in the determination of what it means to be autistic, for individuals, for families and for society.'* (Nadesan, 2005: 2)

In the Ecological Systems Theory developed by the psychologist Urie Brofenbrenner (1979), rather than examining the inner environment of the child, psychological development is seen within a context of wider social systems working at four levels: the microsystem (the immediate social environments that people inhabit), the mesosystem (where two microsystems interact), the exosystem (a broader social context which indirectly influences development), and the macrosystem (the wider social context). This theory forms a framework within which one can examine various levels of social context in the study of autism. Within the field of autism, there is a growing concern regarding listening to autistic voices from a phenomenological perspective (Biklen, 2005) and with regard to the wider social construction of autism (Nadesan, 2005; Timini *et al* 2011). However, the study of autism on a micro-sociological level has been given precious little attention. This paper utilises the theories of Garfinkel (1967) and Goffman (1955; 1959; 1963; 1974) in particular, in order to question current ways of perceiving autism, highlighting issues concerning social interactions involving autistic people, and the stigma of autism, as well as deconstructing the myth of a lack of empathy (Baron-Cohen, 2008; 2011).

Ethnomethodology and autism

The ethnomethodological perspective was first formalised by Garkinkel (1967), as a development from phenomenological theory. The term 'Ethno' referring to the stock of common sense knowledge available to a member of a society (e.g. the rules of a game of noughts and crosses), and Methodology in this instance referring to the methods or strategies that people employ in different settings to make their intended meanings understandable (e.g. turn-taking in conversations). An ethnomethodologist suspends or abandons the belief that an actual social order exists, but rather, suggests that social reality is accomplished and continually constructed by skilled social actors.

Through his breaching experiments, Garfinkel (1967) deliberately violated social reality, in order to shed light on the methods used by people to construct and maintain social reality. Garfinkel (1967) argued that social reality was fragile in nature, and when the natural attitude (the belief that everything is how one thinks it is and others perceive things in much the same way) is breached people are put under a state of stress and do everything in their power to repair the breach. Reactions to breaching can be extreme, yet this also shows the importance people place on maintaining order in their views of the social world.

Rather than lacking a theory of mind, it is argued here that due to differences in the way autistic people process information, they are not socialised into the same shared ethno as neurotypical people, and thus breaches in understanding happen all the time, leaving both in a state of confusion. The difference is that the neurotypical person can repair the breach, by the reassuring belief that approximately 99 out of 100 people still think and act like they do, and remind themselves that they are the normal ones. For McGeer (2004), the theory of mind deficit model of autism is a one-sided asymmetrical view of two people failing to understand one another, with the personal accounts of those diagnosed showing that the supposed lack of subjective awareness of self and others is simply untrue.

The myth of empathy

Ethnomethodologists such as Garfinkel (1967) and Cicourel (1974) suggest that interactions between individuals involve assumptions of normalcy, such as the assumption that others will behave in expected ways, and that when ambiguous meanings are found, they will either be deemed irrelevant to the interaction, or will be immanently explained. Such interpretive procedures involve an inductive logical process, without which an individual would be uncertain of the meaning of the interaction, what was to happen next, and perceiving how others may be experiencing the interaction. According to Durig (1993), the impairments and abilities associated with autism can be seen with regard to the use of deductive and abductive reasoning, rather than inductive logic. For Durig (1993), deductive intellectual activities involve if-then rules, especially those with a guaranteed outcome, such as numerical calculation, memorising information, or collecting objects, whilst abductive activities involve creativity and imagination. Durig's (1993) classification of autism as a preference/reliance on deductive logic (in particular) as opposed to inductive inference, gives an alternative way to conceptualise Baron-Cohen's (2008) empathising-systemising theory. Rather than a lack of theory of mind or ability to empathise, Durig (1993) suggests that an apparent inability in this area comes from a different way of processing information, which does bear a resemblance to Baron-Cohen's (2008) conceptualisation of autistic strengths coming from an ability for splitting and systemising, yet does not involve the need to use a concept of empathy. This formulation would also suggest that rather than being a core deficit, the appearance of a lack of theory of mind would be a potential consequence of an individual processing interactions with others using deductive, rather than inductive logic.

According to Baron-Cohen (2011), a lack of intent to cause harm can co-exist with zero empathy, and suggests that this is the pattern found with autistic people, suggesting that they are zero positive, rather than zero negative (as he suggests is the case with other neurological labels of pathology). This line of thinking, however, implies that a lack of empathy does not in and of itself lead to criminality or cruelty to others, but the intent to cause harm to others. Thus, if one were able to banish a lack of empathy, one would not banish cruelty. The formulation of zero negative (and thus zero positive) does not make sense however, as the intent to cause harm would require some sense of understanding regarding the existence of others outside of oneself, as well as notions of cause and effect regarding ones actions on others. In other words, cruelty requires cognitive empathy which is said to be lacking in the case of zero negative individuals.

The amount of apparent empathy expressed by an individual (autistic or not) will vary depending on who they are interacting with, and the wider social context, on both their ability to understand the attention of others, and in emotional reactions to this information. It is argued here that empathy is a convenient illusion, and the phenomenon that people speak of when referring to it has more to do with language and a sense of shared cultural meanings/symbols (or their ethno). It can be argued that neuro-typical people have no better understanding of how autistics think, than vice versa (McGeer, 2004). The philosopher

Thomas Nagel (1981) wrote about the impossibility of understanding what it may be like to be a bat, yet this could be expanded to all other creatures, including humans. By looking at the breaching experiments of Garfinkel (1967), one can see the fragile nature of the social reality that people inhabit. Garfinkel argued that people have a tendency to fill in the gaps in their perception in order to gain what they think is a full or whole picture. Due to differences in the way autistic people process information (whether it be monotropism, a weak drive toward central coherence, a lack of mirror neurons, or a lack of long-range connectivity in the brain), this filling of gaps tends not to occur (at least to the same extent). Autistic people have a tendency to be more literal, and work upon what is tangible and present, thus conclusions are reached through available information (without filling in the gaps). It is also interesting to note that these issues may well have been partly recognised in the work of Hans Asperger:

> 'Asperger may have believed that his patients lacked the natural attitude that constitutes the socially shared lifeworld, as understood phenomenologically.' (Nadesan, 2005: 76)

It has been suggested that a theory of mind and empathy are essential to that which makes humans what they are. Thus, the characterisation of autistic people lacking such abilities suggests that they are somewhat less than fully human (Lawson, 2010), and when also linked to criminality and cruelty to others, brings back notions of the atavistic criminal. It is argued here, that depicting autistic people as lacking empathy, is an inaccurate and potentially highly dangerous narrative to pursue.

Us and them

People have a tendency to align themselves to others within their in-group and increase this bond through the denigration of out-groups (Tajfel & Turner, 1979). Within interactions with others of an in-group, it can be easily shown that people have little compassion (or affective empathy) for outsiders. Tajfel and Turner (1979) utilising minimal group experiments found that this denigration also occurred, even when distinctions between groups were arbitrary.

According to the Social Identity Theory of Tajfel and Turner (1979), individuals increase their self-image by identifying positively with a group to which they belong, but also by discriminating against the out-group. Tajfel and Turner (1979) suggested that stereotyping others was a normal cognitive process, in which there is a tendency to group phenomena together. In doing so, the differences between groups are exaggerated, along with similarities to those within the in-group, through a process of categorisation, identification, and comparison.

Link and Phelan (2001) suggest that stigma occurs through four social processes. Firstly, by human difference being labelled, secondly by dominant cultural ideology linking labelled individuals to undesirable characteristics, or negative stereotypes, thirdly a dislocation between groups establishes a distinction between us and them, and lastly labelled individuals experience discrimination and a loss of status. In this conceptualisation, stigma is contingent upon differentials of social power.

Stigma and Autism

Durkheim (1895) was the first sociologist to consider stigma as a social phenomena:

> 'Imagine a society of saints, a perfect cloister of exemplary individuals. Crimes or deviance, properly so-called, will there be unknown; but faults, which appear venial to the layman, will there create the same scandal that the ordinary offense does in ordinary consciousnesses. If then, this society has the power to judge and punish, it will define these acts as criminal (or deviant) and will treat them as such.' (Durkheim, 1895)

In this early functionalist formulation of stigma and deviance, both are viewed as inevitable within human societies, and indeed functional for society in terms of maintaining a moral code of values, supporting the social norms of a society and the stability of society as a whole. Although this view has been criticised from a number of perspectives, it is interesting to note that Durkheim also argued that another function of deviance in society was to challenge society and open up possibilities for social change. For Durkheim, a society with an overly strict moral code of behaviour would be just as dysfunctional as an anomic society with a lack of such a consensus, an idea sadly lacking in much subsequent functionalist or New Right sociological theory (Parsons, 1951; Murray, 1990).

In the field of autism, such a functionalist view of society and an individual's place within it, are often taken for granted, depicting autistic people as a financial burden in need of correction and normalisation. As Timini *et al* (2011) argue, being viewed as normal has become progressively harder to achieve:

> *'The desire to control, amend or even extinguish human behaviours that depart from an increasingly narrow stereotype of normality has bedevilled the history of psychiatry.'* (Timini *et al*, 2011: 8)

Lawson (2008) suggests that the discipline of psychology has largely conditioned social concepts of what it is to be normal, yet also highlights the role of media and big business in maintaining these concepts. Lawson (2008) calls for an expansion of what is considered normal, and suggests that society is intolerant and non-inclusive of difference, preventing the healthy development of a wide population of people. This can be seen as an attempt to reduce the social stigma attached to autism and difference more generally, yet without the abolishment of the label, as is suggested by Timini *et al* (2011). Indeed, it is argued here that such a move would not extinguish discrimination against those currently deemed autistic. This can be shown by a recent study into autistic epidemiology in adults in England (Traolach *et al*, 2011), which found that of those exhibiting autism, none were formally diagnosed. Yet in comparison to non-autistics, were likely to have a lower level of education and employment, and to be more likely to be living in government housing.

According to Cottrell (1942, 1978), an interaction between two individuals involves each participant taking on the role of the other, and adjusting their behaviour to the responses of one another. Thus, an individual needs to both process incoming information, as well as developing a strategy of how to present themselves in a meaningful way. From Plato to Shakespeare, it has often been remarked that human social life is analogous with that of actors on a stage. This dramaturgical analogy was theoretically applied by Erving Goffman (1955, 1959, 1963, 1974) to the study of human interactions. Through this formulation, Goffman (1955, 1959, 1963) argued that social actors were involved in a continuous management of the impressions they give to others. For Goffman (1959, 1963), the ability to manage such impressions is fundamental for an individual to be considered normal by others. Hence, those that exhibit autism, whether diagnosed or not, are likely to be considered abnormal and subsequently stigmatised.

To Goffman (1963), a stigma is an attribute, behaviour, or social category that is socially discrediting to the individual. Goffman (1963) described stigma as the gap between the actual social identity an individual inhabits in lived reality, and the virtual social identity expected of them by an idealised social norm. Those who occupy such a social position can be classified as either discredited or discreditable. Those discredited being those who have had their stigma revealed to others, or who are openly visible. The problem here in terms of impression management, is how to manage social interactions when one knows they are known to hold a stigmatising attribute which can affect interactions with others. For the discreditable, the stigma is not known about, and therefore impression management involves the concealment of stigma (known as passing), and when to reveal information about the attribute and to whom. Goffman (1963) suggests that the stigmatised may well see themselves as normal, yet at the same time will realise that they are different within the presence of normal people. An identity that can cause social shame, and when internalised through a self-fulfilling prophecy (Becker, 1963) can lead to low self-esteem and even self-degradation. In the case of autism, amongst other perceived differences, it is the very ability to manage impressions that is viewed as abnormal and not meeting social expectation. Even those deemed high-functioning and who with a great deal of conscious effort are able to pass as normal, can then be stigmatised as falsely claiming their autistic status, and further disabled by not having their difficulties recognised.

Jones *et al* (1984) expanded Goffman's ideas on stigma to six dimensions: the extent to which a stigma is concealable, whether the stigma becomes more prominent over time, the degree to which the stigma disrupts social interactions, the aesthetics of others reactions to the stigma, the origin of the stigma (birth, accidental, or deliberate), and the danger perceived by others on how the stigma may affect them. Although all of these dimensions can affect autistic people to greater or lesser degrees, two of them are of particular interest: obviously, stigma that disrupts social interactions, yet increasingly, the stigma of perceived danger which can be linked to notions of a lack of empathy.

Concluding Remarks

This paper has examined aspects of what it is to be autistic from a micro-sociological perspective, highlighting issues of social interaction and stigma. In so doing, it has shown some of the inadequacies of outsider approaches that objectify the autistic subject from normative/functionalist perspectives, in particular the pernicious view of autistic people lacking empathy. It is also anticipated that such reflections could lead to research utilising micro-sociological perspectives in conjunction with phenomenological and discursive methods.

References

Baron-Cohen S (2008) *Autism: The facts*. London: Open University Press.

Baron-Cohen, S. (2011) *Zero Degrees of Empathy: A new theory of human cruelty*. London: Penguin.

Becker H (1963) *Outsiders: Studies in the sociology of deviance*. New York: The Free Press.

Biklen D (2005) *Autism and the Myth of the Person Alone*. New York: New York University Press.

Brofenbrenner U (1979) *The Ecology of Human Development*. Cambridge: Harvard University Press.

Cicourel A (1974) *Cognitive Sociology*. Harmondsworth: Penguin.

Cottrell L (1942) The Analysis of Situational Fields in Social Psychology. *American Sociological Review* **7** 370–382.

Cottrell L (1978) George Herbert Mead and Harry Stack Sullivan: an unfinished synthesis. *Psychiatry* **41** (2) 151–162.

Durig A (1993) The Microsociology of Autism [online]. Available at: www.autism-resources.com/papers/microsocialogy_of_autism.txt (accessed September 2017).

Durkheim E (1895/1982) *Rules of Sociological Method*. New York: The Free Press.

Engel G (1977) The need for a new medical model: a challenge for biomedicine, *Science* **196** pp129–136.

Garfinkel H (1967) *Studies in Ethnomethodology*. Englewood Cliffs: Prentice-Hall.

Goffman E (1955) On Face-Work. *Psychiatry* **18** (3) 213–231.

Goffman E (1959) *The Presentation of Self in Everyday Life*. New York: Doubleday.

Goffman E (1963) *Stigma: Notes on the management of a soiled identity*. Harmondsworth: Penguin.

Goffman E (1974) *Frame Analysis An Essay on the Organisation of Experience*. Cambridge: Harvard University Press.

Jones E, Farina A, Hastorf A, Markus H, Miller D & Scott R (1984) *Social Stigma: The psychology of marked relationships*. New York: Freeman.

Knapp M, Romeo R & Beecham J (2009) Economic cost of autism in the UK. *Autism* **13** (3) 317–336.

Lawson W (2008) *Concepts of Normality: The autistic and typical spectrum*. London: Jessica Kingsley.

Lawson W (2010) *The Passionate Mind: How people with autism learn*. London: Jessica Kingsley.

Link B & Phelan J (2001) Conceptualizing stigma. *Annual Review of Sociology* **27** 363–385.

McGeer V (2004) Autistic Self-awareness. *Philosophy, Psychiatry and Psychology* **11** 235–251.

Murray C (1990) *The Emerging British Underclass*. London: Institute of Economic Affairs.

Nadesan M (2005) *Constructing Autism: Unravelling the truth and understanding the social*. Abingdon: Routledge.

Nagel T (1981) What is it like to be a bat? In: D Hofstadter and D Dennett (eds) *The Minds I*. London: Penguin.

Parsons T (1951) *The Social System*. New York: Free Press.

Pilgrim D (2002) The biopsychosocial model in Anglo-American psychiatry: past, present and future. *Journal of Mental Health* **11** (6) 585–594.

Tajfel H & Turner J (1979) An integrative theory of intergroup conflict. In: W Austin and S Worchel (eds) *The Social Psychology of Intergroup Relations*. Monterey: Brooks-Cole.

Timini S, Gardner N & McCabe B (2011) *The Myth of Autism*. Basingstoke: Palgrave.

Traolach S, McManus S, Bankart J, Scott F, Purdon S, Smith J, Bebbington P, Jenkins R & Meltzer H (2011) Epidemiology of autism spectrum disorders in adults in the community in England. *Archive of General Psychiatry* **68** (5) 459–465.

So what exactly are autism interventions intervening with?

This article was first published in Good Autism Practice 15 (2): 6-14 in 2014.

Introduction

A cursory look on an internet search engine regarding autism will soon have the viewer coming across the notion of intervention, and in particular a narrative of early intervention to help the development of autistic people. Today, the Research Autism website lists over one-thousand named interventions in the field of autism, along with indications of the amount of research evidence there is to support the claims they make. Yet, with so many on the market, it is quite obvious that they are not all trying to achieve the same goals. With discussions regarding intervention, what is often left out is:

- What is it all for?

- What is one trying to achieve and why?

- Are there ethical issues regarding these purposes, or the means by which one tries to achieve them?

This paper gives an overview of the spectrum of ideology underlying current debates in the field, and the tensions that exist between different viewpoints. I use a number of research studies in the area to highlight these tensions and why they exist by reviewing a number of currently popular practices (e.g. Applied Behavioral Analysis (ABA) (e.g. Lovaas, 1987), Relationship Development Intervention (RDI) (Gutstein & Sheely, 2002) and Intensive Interaction (see www.phoebecaldwell.co.uk and Nind & Hewett, 1994)), and will offer some suggestions as to a way forward that is more open about such disputes, rather than trying to build a false consensus between them.

A conflict of interests

First, it needs to be pointed out that I, like everyone else working in the field of autism, am biased by my own experiences. These being, that I am someone who is on the autism spectrum themselves and also a parent to an autistic child, as well as a person with training in a number of academic disciplines. My work is often critical of established models of practice in the field of autism, particularly those based on behaviourism (Milton & Moon, 2012). As I will attempt to show in this article however, such biases are perhaps inevitable, as they are founded upon some fundamental questions about our philosophy of life, what it is to be human, a social being, to learn, and what it is that one ought to be learning, and so on. Secondly, this leads on to a second kind of 'conflict of interests' within the field of autism, that is, that there are great tensions and controversies between different points of view, often between people who passionately believe in the approach that they are taking and the supposed benefits that taking such an approach can bring. Often, however, such debates and discussions are hidden from view, as if all those involved in the field are in general agreement or consensus. Yet to what extent is a consensus possible? What aspects of learning are there any level of agreement about? What are the main areas of tension and why do they exist? In this paper, I hope to explore these issues.

Theories of learning

Early on in teacher training courses, students are introduced to a number of theories of learning. These provide conceptual frameworks within which to try and understand how learning takes place (Merriam & Caffarella, 1991: 138),

Although any such breakdown gives a generalised overview of such theories and not an in-depth understanding, one can see that there are a number of ways of viewing learning, what the purpose of education is, and how best to achieve the outcomes one aspires to.

Behaviourists following Skinner see learning largely in terms of conditioning through external stimuli that is processed as either something negative or something positive, reinforcing or extinguishing behaviours from being repeated. Cognitivist theory looks more closely at the attributes of the learner rather than making changes in the environment to influence behaviour. Humanists emphasise subjective understandings, while social constructivists suggest that learning should be a mutual and tailored process of construction. In practice, a teacher may use a mixture of the above approaches, whilst others may be more devoted to a particular approach.

This spread of views is also found across the field of intervention research and practice with autistic children.

Applied Behavioural Analysis (ABA)

'Viewing autism as a list of deficits that can be corrected through a series of discrete trials will not make an autistic person any less autistic. Teaching autistic people how to 'pass' so they can blend in better with non autistics is similar to the belief that a closed gay person will live a happier and more fulfilled life by being closeted than someone who is 'out'.' (Zurcher, 2012)

When studying the field of autism, the influence of behaviourism as a theory of learning can appear dominant, through the work of Lovaas (1987) to contemporary debates regarding autism interventions, such as the documentary *Autism: challenging behaviour* that was aired on BBC4 in 2013 (Two Step Films, 2013). Those researching autism for the first time will come across a plethora of interventions generally based upon the principles of Applied Behavioural Analysis (ABA). According to the NHS guidelines for autism treatments (NHS, 2014), ABA is said to be based on the breaking down of skills into small tasks in a highly structured way, and reinforcing behaviour thought to be positive, while discouraging behaviour deemed inappropriate. ABA programmes are then described as an intensive therapy of 40 hours of work a week, over a number of years. This intensity is not followed by all theorists or practitioners who support ABA methods though. It should be noted that there is a vast array of approaches that have been influenced by ABA and many of them are at odds with one another in various respects. For instance, the early aversive punishments used by Lovaas (1987) and colleagues, and their goal of making autistic children 'indistinguishable from their peers' are now largely and rightly frowned upon. One popular approach, especially in America, is that of Early Intensive Behavioural Intervention (EIBI). This intervention often uses the method of 'discrete trial learning', used it is said, to build foundational learning skills. The behaviour of children is subjected to a functional assessment, where the teacher describes a 'problem behaviour', identifies antecedents for why the behaviour is occurring, and analyses the consequences of the behaviour. This analysis is thought to indicate what influences and sustains such behaviours. Other methods include Pivotal Response Therapy (PRT) which attempts to use behaviourist principles in more naturalistic settings, where 'natural reinforcers' such as a favourite toy are preferred to rewards such as a chocolate treat.

Despite widespread support and the mounting piles of research papers extolling the virtues of ABA-based practices of various iterations, such approaches have also come under much criticism from scientists, ethicists, autistic people and their families. ABA, like many other therapies and interventions purported to help autistic people, is often sold as if it is a 'miracle treatment', and if not, as the only recognised approach to be 'scientifically proven', and needed as quickly as possible in order not to miss the 'window of opportunity'. One of the clearest examples of such an extreme position can be seen in the account of ABA given by Maurice (1994). In her book entitled, *Let Me Hear Your Voice: A family's triumph over autism*, she claims that ABA had saved her children's lives, likening it to chemotherapy as a treatment for cancer. Whatever approach favoured, it is important that such zealotry be avoided by practitioners working with autistic children. Since, in my view, it will lead to poor practice, as Ariane Zurcher (2012), a mother of an autistic child describes:

> '...when she did not show the sort of monumental leaps promised, the ABA therapists said it was because we were at fault. Never once did any of the therapists, supervisor or agency waver in their firm belief that ABA was a solid, 'scientifically' backed methodology. It was spoken of as fact.' (Zurcher, 2012)

Similarly, John Lubbock (2001), in the UK, the father of a boy with autism who followed an ABA programme, whilst an advocate of the principles of ABA was critical of the fact that often the therapists and some of the supervisors, 'had a fundamental lack of wider knowledge and experience' and that this 'will tend to make people inflexible, as they have no response to problems other than more Lovaas.' (p319).

This concern can equally be applied to other interventions where the proponents and/or practitioners only have knowledge of that particular intervention and also sometimes very little knowledge of autism.

In recent years, a North American group of autistic writers began a project entitled the Loud Hands Project (see www.loudhandsproject.org/), named after an online article from an autistic person who critiqued the therapy they had received when younger, and the request for 'quiet hands'. One of the biggest criticisms made of behaviourist approaches is that the behaviours deemed as either positive or negative are being decided upon by non-autistic others, often with little idea of what it is subjectively like to be autistic, or to have an unusual autistic learning style. Methods such as discrete trials can be intensive to the extent of being overloading, particularly when staged in a face-to-face manner, and distress can be ignored when viewed as inappropriate behaviour. When concentrating on outward behaviour, it is essential (in my view) that practitioners do not forget about autistic cognition and subjective understandings, and how these influence one's interactions with the social situations one finds oneself in. One area of ABA-based theory and practice which states clearly that they are against notions of cure and normalisation is that of Positive Behaviour Support (PBS), yet it is still open to the criticism of who gets to decide what is and what is not positive about behaviour, and that perhaps some of the nuances of these ideas are lost on many people practising ABA in the hope of some kind of miracle transformation. As an example, I would recommend watching the parental narratives in the film *Autism: challenging behaviour* (2013).

The phrases 'scientifically proven' and 'evidence-based' often used in pro-ABA literature also need to be critiqued. Gernsbacher (2003), for example, reviewed these exaggerated claims within the field, as well as showing the flaws in the often cited article by Lovaas (1987). More recently, Michelle Dawson (2007) has critiqued the methodology of ABA-related research, and a number of reviews and studies have shown no significant difference between ABA-based approaches and other approaches (Magiati *et al,* 2007; Fernandes & Amato, 2013; Boyd *et al*, 2014). Hogsbro (2011) compared the progression of children on the autism spectrum receiving ABA programmes, with those in ordinary placements, specialist autism day-care units, and those receiving a mixture of provision. Hogsbro utilised measures often used by studies that had found positive gains from ABA, such as IQ scores, and measurements for language comprehension, self-help skills, and the capacity for social contact. Hogsbro found that on average, the ABA provision had a negative impact on all of these factors, and the group which performed best were those receiving support from 'specialist autism units'. This study also looked into parental and professional attitudes toward the provision the children were receiving, and found that within the ABA group, the parents had the highest expectations for their children, and that professionals and parents using this model subjectively rated improvements in these areas higher than all of the other groups. Such evidence raises questions as to the validity of anecdotal accounts of change, yet also with accounts that suggest the ABA is a 'proven' method or indeed 'medical treatment'. Hopefully such findings will lead to research into the common factors between approaches, beneficial factors within them, and influential factors such as maturation which have little to do with what educational approach one takes.

Relationship and developmental approaches

Discussions regarding autism interventions often refer to alternatives to behavioural approaches as relationship-based or developmental approaches. This is a very broad category however which encompasses a number of differing approaches, most with a strong cognitivist or functionalist basis (looking at levels of psychological and social functioning, often compared to normative averages), yet also often using humanist and / or social or situational ideas. Also, with the so-called cognitive revolution in psychology, one could say that there has been a general shift in education theory toward a cognitivist approach, such as that derived from the work of Piaget (1896/1980). Such theories often look at measurements of functioning against normative (average) stages of development. Indeed, one can see elements of a functionalist perspective in some behaviourist narratives, particularly PBS. Piaget also highlighted peer relations and active learning experiences. Social or situational approaches however, often draw upon the ideas of Vygotsky (1896 – 1934) who looked at learning as a socially situated process, and saw the teacher as more involved in scaffolding learning for their pupils/students. Ideas originating from both these theorists, and indeed those of humanist theorists, can be found within the theoretical explanations of a number of autism interventions. One firmly established cognitivist approach is that of TEACCH (Treatment and Education of Autistic and Communication handicapped CHildren) or structured teaching (Schopler & Mesibov, 1995). This approach places emphasis on the structure and predictable sequencing of activities, as well as visual schedules and prompts. More recently the Social Communication, Emotional Regulation and Transactional Support (SCERTS) approach (Prizant *et al,* 2002) has been formulated, that looks to be a child and family-centred approach, and highlights the development of 'functional' social communication, regulating emotions, and mutual transactional support.

Some approaches highlight the building of relationships with others as the primary focus for attention. Early examples would include the Option or Son-Rise programme (Kaufman, 1994), often criticised for its outlandish claims of miracle cure and high cost of the programme for parents, and the floortime approach developed by Greenspan (see www.stanleygreenspan. com). This approach focuses on the sensory differences experienced by autistic people, and in following the child's lead and interests, rather than being adult-led. A somewhat more humanistic approach, it still however keeps a foot in the functionalist camp by suggesting that the approach helps children to climb the 'developmental ladder', conceived as operating in a number of stages. Like other approaches, its starting point is a view regarding autistic 'deficits', in this case deemed to be disturbances in the sensory system, motor planning, communication, relating to others, and an inability to connect one's desire to intentional action.

While there are elements of truth in seeing these areas as those found difficult by autistic people, an entirely deficit model of what autism is, has its own disadvantages (see later in this paper). It is the view of the proponents of this approach that autistic people miss out on stages of development, yet such progress can be re-strengthened by meaningful interactions and play with caregivers. Relationship Development Intervention (RDI) shares many similarities in theory and practice with the floortime approach, in terms of 'functional relationships' being the main aim of the intervention. This programme is based on the concept that autistic people are deficient in what is termed 'dynamic intelligence', a somewhat umbrella term that includes thinking flexibly, theory of mind, coping with change, and processing more than one piece of information at the same time. By working upon these qualities, those who follow RDI suggest that the quality of life for children on the autism spectrum can improve. Unfortunately, RDI supporters seem to have fallen into the same trap as previous approaches, with large claims being made from scant evidence. Also, the use of the term 'dynamic thinking' can be criticised for being too all-encompassing a term, especially when others have used the exact same words to describe a more direct and sensory experience of one's environment (Pirsig, 1991).

Finally, there is the approach of intensive interaction. Similar to floortime and RDI, it is a relationship-based model, which seeks to make functional gains in communication. However, the focus here is primarily building trust and rapport on the child's own terms. This approach is the one that I personally favour, and a fine exponent of this approach would be Phoebe Caldwell (for more information, see www.phoebecaldwell.co.uk). An issue with all of these approaches is that the scientific evidence (mentioned earlier) does not seem to favour any approach, at least not in terms of making significant changes in communication (often a key target that approaches share). Studies show massive variance in terms of the outcomes of interventions, whatever the purpose they are set to. There is certainly not enough evidence for me to suggest one over another as a one-size-fits-all approach. Thus, I would recommend avoiding taking such a stance, whatever one's leanings may be in favour of one approach or another. More research is needed too, to see if there are any active factors that do make a significant difference. Yet, such studies should also involve the views of autistic people and their families regarding what one wishes to intervene with in the first place. Perhaps with its model of mutual respect in interactions, engaging with autistic interests, and taking into account autistic cognition and sensory differences, it is little wonder that I find intensive interaction the most favourable of current approaches for children on the autism spectrum.

The concept of neurodiversity and its implications

Instead of trying to give a full account of the history of the concepts of neurodiversity and self-advocacy, given one would be trying to account for over two decades of culture, I will give my own understanding of neurodiversity as someone who identifies as autistic. For me, the concept of neurodiversity suggests that variations in neurological development are part of natural diversity, rather than something to be pathologised using a purely medical model of disability, defined by one's deviation from statistical or idealised norms of observed behaviour. This is not to say that those who identify as autistic people or other forms of neuro-identity do not find life challenging.

> *'Extremes of any combination come to be seen as 'psychiatric deviance'. In the argument presented here, where disorder begins is entirely down to social convention, and where one decides to draw the line across the spectrum.'* (Milton, 1999, unpublished masters dissertation)

Spectrum in this case refers to the 'human spectrum of dispositional diversity'.

Embedded in more of a social model of disability (see Milton, 2012), such a conceptualisation of neurodiversity would suggest that autistic people are significantly disadvantaged in many aspects of life. Such a concept is not devoid of an understanding of embodied differences, indeed far from it, yet is a socially situated understanding of such differences. Other than from autistic scholars, such conceptualisations are rarely given much credence outside of the disciplines of sociology and critical disability studies. When looking at an educational programme that best suits such a conceptualisation, it is evident that one would favour one that did not focus on perceived deficits, less still behaviours deemed inappropriate. What would be highlighted would be an understanding of differing dispositions, a building of relationships in a respectful manner, engaging with an individual's abilities and interests and not just what they find difficult. Is this not how many people, whatever their disposition, would like to be treated within educational settings? For me, the closest any of the previously discussed approaches gets to such a social/situational approach is intensive interaction, particularly the variations and practice demonstrated by Phoebe Caldwell. Does this mean that one should accept these methods as something to blueprint and reproduce everywhere? No. It does however, call into question whether any educational approach will ever be able to claim a stronger evidence-base than any other, as autistic voices keep saying – one-size does not fit all. Thus, for me, none can claim to have a scientific evidence base of effectiveness. For me, this has not been demonstrated, and is unlikely ever to be.

Tensions in the field reaching a tipping point?

Recently, Professor Simon Baron-Cohen (2014) posted an article in an online magazine in response to what he would like to see retired as a scientific concept. His answer to this question was 'radical behaviourism', the form of behaviourism proposed by BF Skinner that is still influential upon ABA-based practices today. In this article, Baron-Cohen (2014) only alludes to the field of autism, without directly mentioning it. Given his work in the field of autism, however, one could view this as a political act. I did not find it at all surprising that he should disagree with behaviourist ideas, given that one could describe his theories as based more within the cognitivist-functionalist camp. What was perhaps more surprising was that this article followed on from the publication of the NICE guidelines on intervention for autism in adulthood (NICE, 2012), which contained aspects of behaviourist theory, yet whose committee was chaired by Baron-Cohen. The article led to a stream of rebukes from behaviourist academics and practitioners, with one commentator giving him a C+ for his understanding if it was an undergraduate essay.

In the defence of Baron-Cohen (2014), I believe he used the word 'scientifically' in exchange for theoretically, in order to appeal to a lay audience, and that his references of animal behaviours could have been used as a metaphor for the treatment of autistic people (both aspects of his article that were criticised, among others). As someone who favours a more sociological and social constructivist (social/situational) view of education and learning, I would have disagreements with both behaviourists and Baron-Cohen (2014), and this is the point: consensus in this field is about as likely as having a sustained political consensus between all political interest groups, from fascists to communists. The reason such a consensus is not possible, is because the debates are largely theoretical and ideological. Thus, there will not be any agreement regarding how to measure progress, or even if one can. The most important message here for parents and practitioners working with autistic children is that there are no easy answers!

Concluding comments: what is a parent or practitioner working with autistic children to do?

The answer to this question is never an easy one. Due to the diversity of dispositions and learning styles of people on the autism spectrum, asking 'what works?' in an educational setting, is like asking the same question about people who are not autistic. Thus, the common sense answer is: it depends on the child, what you are trying to teach and why, the environment one is in and the skills, expertise and personal style of teachers and parents. One thing that does not work though, speaking as an autistic person, is trying to 'cure' someone of being autistic. Autism is a description of someone's cognition, the way they behave, their way of being and acting in the world. Thus, I prefer to call myself an autistic person, yet do not see autism as a cluster of behavioural deficits to be fixed.

'We need to see the world from the autistic perspective and apply approaches based on a mutuality of understanding that are rational and ethical – which respect the right of the individual to be different – yet recognises and deals with distress and offers practical help. We should encourage and motivate the person to develop strengths rather than focus on 'deficits'. This will mean offering opportunity for development while supporting emotional stability.' (Mills, 2013)

The National Autistic Society (NAS) promotes what it calls a framework, rather than an approach, known as SPELL (Structure, Positive, Empathy, Low-arousal, Links). The first aspect of this framework is 'structure'. This is an often cited area of need for autistic people, often assumed to be deficient in executive functioning (by some cognitivists), yet it is a part of any educational planning. Imposing structures that are not needed or indeed impinge on learning is something to be avoided, and care must be taken that structures are put in place that promote the autonomy of the learner and reduce their stress (not increase it!). Being 'positive' relates to focusing not only on what a learner finds challenging, but what they find interesting, or that they have an aptitude for. Self-esteem and self-worth can be badly affected by attempts to normalise one's differences (Milton & Moon, 2012), thus the old proposed goal of making autistic people 'indistinguishable from their peers' (Lovaas, 1987) needs to be jettisoned. 'Empathy' may sound a great deal simpler than it actually is in practice.

It is often commented that autistic people have a deficient theory of mind, yet how accurate are non-autistic theories of autistic minds? For me, due to dispositional and cultural differences, a 'double empathy problem' exists (Milton, 2012), that is, that both parties can have difficulties in understanding one another. Bridging this gap can take much will and effort from both parties, plus the building of a strong trusting relationship. Again, I would refer here to the work of Phoebe Caldwell (www.phoebecaldwell.co.uk). A 'low-arousal' approach is one that recognises the harmful effects of stress and thus seeks to reduce confrontations and sensory overload. It should be remembered though that low-arousal does not mean no-arousal and that some sensory activities can be great fun too (although favoured activities may vary widely from one person to the next). The 'links' aspect of this approach states that parents, other agencies and so on, work in collaboration and with consistency and respect. For more information on the SPELL framework, information about approaches and current evidence and research, I would advise parents and practitioners to look at the Research Autism website (2014) and Mills (2013).

Last but by no means least, in the words of Douglas Adams and the *Hitchhiker's Guide to the Galaxy:* 'Don't Panic!'

References

Baron-Cohen S (2014) *Radical Behaviourism* [online]. Available at: www.edge.org/response-detail/25473 (accessed September 2017).

Boyd B, Hume K, McBee M, Alessandri M, Gutierrez A, Johnson L, Sperry L & Odom SL (2014) Comparative efficacy of LEAP, TEACCH and non-model-specific special education programs for preschoolers with autism spectrum disorders. *Journal of Autism and Developmental Disorders* **44** (2) 366–380.

Dawson M (2007) *A Tale of Two ABA Studies* [online]. Available at: http://autismcrisis.blogspot.co.uk/2007/06/tale-of-two-aba-studies.html (accessed September 2017).

Fernandes FD & Amato C (2013) Applied Behaviour Analysis and autism spectrum disorders: literature review. *CoDAS* **25** (3) 289–296.

Gernsbacher M (2003) Is one style of early behavioural treatment for autism 'scientifically proven'? University of Wisconsin-Madison.

Gutstein SE & Sheely RK (2002) *Relationship Development Intervention with Young Children.* London: Jessica Kingsley Publishers.

Hogsbro K (2011) *Ethical consideration following an evaluation of preschool programs for children with autism spectrum disorders* [online]. Available at: www.soc.aau.dk/fileadmin/user_upload/kbm/VoF/Kurser/2011/evidence/Kjeld-H-Ethical-consideration-following-an-evaluation-of-preshool.pdf (accessed 11 February, 2014).

Jordan R Jones G & Murray D (1998) *Educational interventions for children with autism: a literature review of recent and current research*. Report 77 Sudbury: DfEE.

Kaufman B (1994) *Son Rise: The miracle continues*. California: HJ Kramer.

Lovaas O (1987) Behavioural treatment and normal educational and intellectual functioning in young autistic children. *Journal of Consulting and Clinical Psychology* **55** 3–9.

Lubbock J (2001) In the balance: the Lovaas experience. In: J Richer and S Coates (Eds) *Autism: In search of coherence*. London: Jessica Kingsley Publishers.

Magiati I, Charman T & Howlin P (2007) A two-year prospective follow-up study of community-based early intensive behavioural intervention and specialist nursery provision for children with autism spectrum disorders. *Journal of Child Psychology and Psychiatry* **48** (8) 803–812.

Maurice C (1994) *Let Me Hear Your Voice: A family's triumph over autism*. London: Ballantine Books.

Merriam S & Caffarella R (1991) *Learning in Adulthood*. Oxford: Jossey-Bass Publishers.

Mills R (2013) *Guidance for considering a treatment approach in autism* [online]. Available at: http://researchautism-interventions/making-the-decision/intervention-questions (accessed February 2014).

Milton D (1999) *The Rise of Psychopharmacology* (unpublished). Masters essay, University of London.

Milton D (2012a) *So What Exactly is Autism?* Resource within AET National. Standards, London: Autism Education Trust.

Milton D (2012b) On the ontological status of autism: the 'double empathy problem'. *Disability and Society* **27** (6) 883–887.

Milton D & Moon L (2012) The normalisation agenda and the psycho-emotional disablement of autistic people. *Autonomy* **1** (1).

National Health Service (2014) *Treating Autism and Asperger Syndrome* [online]. Available at: www.nhs.uk/Conditions/Autistic-spectrum-disorder/Pages/Treatment.aspx (accessed September 2017).

NICE (2014) *Autism Spectrum Disorder in Adults: Diagnosis and management* [online]. www.nice.org.uk/guidance/CG142 (accessed September 2017).

Nind M & Hewett D (1994) *Access to Communication*. London: David Fulton.

Parsons S, Guldberg K, MacLeod A & Jones G (2009) *International review of the literature of evidence of best practice provision in the education of persons with autistic spectrum disorders*. Dublin: NCSE.

Pirsig R (1991) *Lila: An inquiry into morals*. London: Alma Books.

Prizant BM, Wetherby AM, Rubin E & Laurent AC (2002) The SCERTS model: enhancing communication and socioemotional abilities of children with autism spectrum disorders. *Jenison Autism Journal* **14** 2–19.

Schopler E & Mesibov G (1995) *Learning and Cognition in Autism.* New York: Plenum Press.

Vermeulen P (2014) *The practice of promoting happiness in autism*, In: Jones G and Hurley E (eds) *Good Autism Practice: Autism, happiness and well-being* Birmingham: BILD.

Two Step Films (2013) *Autism: Challenging Behaviour* (2013), Two Step Films.

Zurcher A (2012) *Tackling that Troublesome Issue of ABA and Ethics* [online]. Available at: http://emmashopebook.com/2012/10/10/tackling-that-troublesome-issue-of-aba-and-ethics/ (accessed September 2017).

Tracing the influence of Fernand Deligny on autism studies

This essay is derived in part from an article published in Disability &
Society on 15 Mar 2016, available online: http://wwww.tandfonline.com/
http://dx.doi.org/10.1080/09687599.2016.1186529

Abstract

In recent years, I have had a growing interest in the work of Deleuze and Guattari, the influence of Fernand Deligny's work on their own, and the similarities and differences between their respective philosophies and those within my own writings as an autistic academic and activist. Recently a translation of Deligny's writing became available. Deligny's writing, even when translated, is not easy to decipher, and perhaps reflects his 'rhizome-esque' philosophy and practice. Yet according to Burk there were three main principals which characterised the work of Deligny: the network as a mode of being (called the 'Arachnean'); the art of acting and doing from which his methodology of 'mapping' attempted to trace; and, lastly, the 'primordial communism' of a shared common site of living. In this article, these themes will be explored and contrasted with the theoretical writings of the autistic author Jim Sinclair and those of my own, as well as indicating how they influenced the concepts later devised by Deleuze and Guattari.

Introduction

Starting in the 1950s, Deligny and his co-workers collectively ran residential communes in France for autistic children and young people, who otherwise would have been institutionalised (Hilton, 2015). Deligny also rejected the dominance of psychoanalytic theory and practice that often permeated (and continues to permeate) cultural attitudes to autism within Francophone nations:

> 'For me, psychoanalysis is a curiously foreign language … And
> then I got used to it, all the more easily when I met an autistic

individual who, clearly, could no more understand our language than I could psychoanalysis.' (Deligny, 2015: 171)

According to Burk (2013) there were three main principals which characterised the work of Deligny: the network as a mode of being (called the 'Arachnean'); the art of acting and doing from which his methodology of 'mapping' attempted to trace; and, lastly, the 'primordial communism' of a shared common site of living. In this article, these themes will be explored and contrasted with the theoretical writings of the autistic author Jim Sinclair (1993) and those of my own (Milton, 2012; 2013; 2014a; 2014b; 2014c), as well as indicating how they influenced the concepts later devised by Deleuze and Guattari (1972;1980).

The network as a mode of being

Deligny writes of the 'Humans-that-we-are', a kind of idealised functional state of normative humanity, as a destructive hegemonic discourse, and also as an invented symbolic mythology or fantastical projection. Contrasted with the 'Humans-that-we-are' are presented human beings as gesture and form, a kind of pre-lingual purity exemplified by the way of being and acting of the autistic young people he worked and lived with:

I shall say the same thing about the mode of being in a network, which is perhaps the very nature of human beings, 'the mind' merely intervening into the bargain, in this case, and its work is the excess rather than the structure of the network. (Deligny, 2015). Deligny further contrasts the symbolic point of view of the 'Humans-that-we-are' against the point of seeing of autistic young people, conceived to be an immediate sensory process. Deligny likens the way of being of an autistic person to a being without consciousness of self and other, not being conscious of being 'woven in language'. In this way, Deligny sets a binary distinction between the non-verbal autistic world, inhabiting a pre-lingual 'network', and the symbolic world of language. This description shares similarities with descriptions of autistic ways of being and acting in the world made by Milton (2012; 2013; 2014a; 2014b; 2014c), yet rather than describing a spectrum of tendencies toward either extreme as Milton does, Deligny presents an almost 'ideal type' model of these differences, perhaps in order to theoretically juxtapose them, but also no doubt influenced by his working with autistic people who lived largely beyond the realm of language (or at least verbal expression in speech). For Deligny, however, denying the autistic person access (theoretically) to the 'thought-out-project' or the fantasy of neat outcomes pursued by the 'Humans-that-we-are' may be some kind of saving grace:

> *'… I inflict this right on them and condemn them a likeness – an identity – that is all the more burdensome because it is fictitious. Certainly, they have a right to the higher level; but what can they do with this right, if not live the disarray of extravagating, which literally means to wander off the path? What path are we talking about? The path of the thought-out project.'* (Deligny, 2015: 50)

For Deligny, despite the dogmatic pursuit of the 'Humans-that-we-are' which is imposed onto autistic people, autistic people would continue to operate in the mode of being of the network. Deligny also asked whether the 'Humans-that-we-are' are deprived of access to acting in the present without symbolic referents to depend upon; and if so, if this was a steep price to pay for pursuing the 'thought-out-project'. It is certainly of interest that Deligny imagined a mode of being outside of notions of self and auto-biographical narrative that have later been reflected in the writings of autistic authors such as Milton (2014c), who conceived of the 'aut-ethnography', involving the telling of a fragmented and rhizome-esque story as opposed to a coherent narrative of selfhood over time (as is often the case in auto-ethnographies).

The 'Arachnean' analogy

In order for networks as a mode of being to grow and propagate, humans – like any other creature – must make use of the coincidences of their environments for their own purposes. As an example, a spider must find something to attach its web to:

> *'… the network being nothing more than 'a permanent or accidental assemblage of interwoven lines.'* (Deligny, 2015: 77)

Throughout Deligny's writing, he makes an analogy with the network as a mode of being with the life of the spider and the weaving of a web. In using such an analogy, he suggests that the existence of networks is in constant danger of falling apart, or else becoming a constraining institution:

> *'A network can complete itself by disappearing or by becoming an institution. The sole underpinning that allows for a network is a breach, a rift.'* (Deligny, 2015: 46)

The notion of lines of flight becoming 'clumped' and reified in institutional form has also been a topic addressed by autistic authors in recent times

(Milton, 2013). One can also easily see the striking influence Deligny had on Deleuze and Guattari's (1972; 1980) concept of the rhizome, but also the notions of a 'plane of immanence' and a 'body-without-organs'.

Deligny's maps

Deligny used a method of making ongoing 'maps' of the wander lines (tracing the movements over time) of the autistic people he lived and worked with. These maps were not seen as completed products but continuous works in progress, with traces of the movements of the autistic people being layered upon each other over a number of years, because it was not a finished product which was the object of the exercise but the exercise of tracing and mapping itself. Deligny envisioned these maps as inscriptions of a way of being and acting in the world, the mode of being of the Arachnean network, a pure form of humanity acting without the purpose of a 'thought-out-project'.

In explaining these maps, Deligny refers to an example of Aboriginal art from northern Australia, where a painting of a turtle is made on a piece of bark. Whilst the turtle painting is meticulously made, once 'finished' it is then discarded, with the meaning of the exercise being in the making, the process, and not the product. Of course, being seen as unproductive could have its difficulties when viewed by the 'Humans-that-we-are':

> *'An autistic child traces; you can always ask yourself what, and answer your own question in the same breath.'* (Deligny, 2015: 93)

The maps were seen as interactive living entities, not static pieces of art to make a coherent meaning from – like the Aboriginal art Deligny cites – and yet also as a way of attempting to engage with the way of being of non-verbal autistic people.

Primordial communism

Deligny utilised the term 'primordial communism' to describe the way of living he experienced, not trying to evoke an historical period but in terms of that which formulates an origin. In this sense, Deligny saw the network as more fundamental to human existence than language, yet as destroyed by language and the 'thought-out-project':

> *'To communicate? I understand well, or rather the word, as I understand it is doubled … In order to make the tacit speak, what is required is to want, to do violence and to violate, and not at all a secret or something that would resist being said.'* (Deligny, 2015: 91)

For Deligny, the network as a way of being is outside of language, and thus by naming it one is somewhat doing violence to it:

> *'We could have been led to an over-abundance of comprehension, which is often what happens to these children …'* (Deligny, 2015: 156)

In seeking to gain a commonality with the autistic people he and his colleagues worked and lived with, Deligny used the term 'topos' or the local environment and affordances of living, a place which to Deligny appeared resistant to being fully comprehended. Yet by mapping the wander lines of autistic people over many years, Deligny argued this allowed them to see (yet not comprehend) something else, something of the network at play, with the intersections of the wander lines (what Milton, 2013 referred to as 'clumping'), showing an underlying commonality and mode of being of the network.

Conclusion

Deligny asks us to imagine a mode of being and relating to others, without imposing on autistic people the need to be like the 'Humans-that-we-are', a functioning whole subject or 'thought-out-project'. Nothing could stand in stronger contrast to the notion that one needs to find out what the function of autistic behaviour is, or what autistic behaviour is trying to communicate. Indeed, Deligny's view could be seen as anti-interventionist if one considers the main aim of many autism interventions to be remedial in focus:

> *'To respect the autistic being is not to respect the being that he or she would be as other; it is to do what is needed so the network can weave itself.'* (Deligny, 2015: 111)

Several decades before the growth of the neurodiversity movement, Deligny and his collaborators were rejecting notions of autism as a pathological deviation from the norm, and instead were:

> *'… in search of a practice that would exclude from the outset interpretations referring to some code; we did not take the children's way of being as scrambled, coded messages addressed to us.'* (Deligny, 2015: 79)

A statement reminiscent of the seminal work of autistic activist Jim Sinclair:

> *'Grant me the dignity of meeting me on my own terms … Recognise that we are equally alien to each other, that my ways of being are not merely damaged versions of yours. Question your assumptions. Define your terms. Work with me to build bridges between us.'* (Sinclair, 1993)

Whether or not one agrees with the philosophical notions Deligny helped to conceive of and inspire, the similarities with the work of autistic authors, alongside his influence on the work of Deleuze and Guattari (1972; 1980), are striking, and indicate that the network he began to weave all those years ago continues to develop and grow, like a rhizome, but in the shadows.

Disclosure statement

No potential conflict of interest was reported by the author.

References

Burk D (2013) *Living Network Ecologies: A triptych on the universe of Fernand Deligny* [online]. Available at: https://sites.fhi.duke.edu/ecologyofnetworks/2013/04/23/living-network-ecologies-a-triptych-on-the-universe-of-fernand-deligny/ (accessed September 2017).

Deleuze G & F Guattari (1972) *Anti-Oedipus*. Translated by Robert Hurley, Mark Seem and Helen Lane, 1977. New York: Viking.

Deleuze G & F Guattari (1980) *A Thousand Plateaus*. Translated by Brain Massumi, 1987. Minneapolis: University of Minnesota Press.

Deligny F (2015) *The Arachnean and Other Texts*. Translated by Drew S Burk and Catherine Porter, 2015. Minneapolis: Univocal publishing.

Hilton L (2015) *Mapping the Wander Lines: The quiet revelations of Fernand Deligny* [online]. Available at: https://lareviewofbooks.org/review/mapping-the-wander-lines-the-quiet-revelations-of-fernand-deligny (accessed September 2017).

Milton D (2012) On the ontological status of autism: the 'double empathy problem. *Disability and Society* **27** (6) 883–887.

Milton D (2013) 'Clumps': an autistic reterritorialisation of the rhizome. *Theorising Normalcy and the Mundane*. 4th International Conference, Sheffield Hallam University, 4 September 2013.

Milton D (2014a) Autistic Expertise: A critical reflection on the production of knowledge in autism studies. *Autism: The International Journal of Research and Practice* **18** (7) 794–802.

Milton D (2014b) Embodied Sociality and the Conditioned Relativism of Dispositional Diversity. *Autonomy, the Critical Journal of Interdisciplinary Autism Studies* **1** (3).

Milton D (2014c) Becoming autistic: an aut-ethnography. *Cutting Edge Psychiatry in Practice* **1** (4) 185–192.

Sinclair J (1993) *Don't Mourn for Us* [online]. Available at: http://www.autreat.com/dont_mourn.html (accessed September 2017).

7 concepts of sociological interest

This article was first published online as part of the #7daysofaction campaign in 2016.

This essay has been inspired by a couple of recent events. Firstly, whilst on a panel discussion at a student study weekend, the question was asked why academics had to use such difficult language. In my response I conceded that academics often confuse people and could make more of an attempt to be accessible, yet also suggested that academic terms were just another form of a 'practice language', where one can learn the meanings and partake in such language if one has access to those utilising such words on a regular basis. I also added that the terms used provided a kind of short-hand to get what would take a paragraph of explanation to get across to other people otherwise. So, in many respects it is up to academics to explain the terms that they are using. Also recently, I posted a comment on twitter with the academic conceptual word 'iatrogenic' contained in it. I received one response, which was what I was hoping for with the original post. This response said they had looked the word up on the internet and agreed with the point I was making. In the spirit of explaining the use of such terms, as an autistic sociologist, what better to apply them to than the social structures of Assessment and Treatment Units (ATUs) at the heart of the #7Daysof action campaign? So, I have chosen seven sociological concepts to explain and show the potential relevance of for such an analysis.

The (degradations of) bureaucracy – Max Weber

To begin this sociological journey, where better to start than with one of the 'founding fathers of sociology' (yeah I know – what about the mothers? Yet, there is a reason for this being historical...): Max Weber. A German academic working over 100 years ago and who, amongst exploring many other topics, was drawn to the increasing way that social institutions were becoming increasingly rationalised. Weber suggested that the establishment of bureaucracies were one of the defining aspects of the then 'modern era'. Only through such large-scale planning could the modern world, as he saw it, be taking the shape that it was. Weber also thought that modern bureaucracies were technically superior to previous forms of administration. Yet, bureaucracy in Weber's analysis was not without its downsides. With the ever increasing rationalisation and ability to 'calculate results', such large-scale organisations became overly constraining when dealing with individual cases ('The computer says no' could be seen as a recent cultural example of this frustration being expressed). The more idiosyncratic and unique the case, the more a bureaucracy would struggle to cope with how to process it. In other words, bureaucracy leads to depersonalisation. The increasing rationalisation of society, Weber thought of as an inescapable trajectory and forecast that the 20th century would be characterised by an 'iron cage of bureaucracy'.

Despite such reservations about the rationalisation of society, Weber proposed an 'ideal type' bureaucracy, regarding how they could be ideally run efficiently. The first aspect of such an organisation Weber saw as formal hierarchy. Whilst I have my own issues with such hierarchical ways of organising people, he envisaged such a structure as the basis of central planning and accountability, with communication up and down the structure also being of importance (the Mazars review I hear you cry – well yes… moving on…). Weber suggested that one needed consistent management of rules, that are then executed across all levels of the organisation (cough!), that work is done by 'specialists' (oops!), that work is organised based on type of work and skills that practitioners have, that organisations can be either 'up-focused' serving those at the top of the organisation, or 'in-focused' serving the organisation itself and those within it (or I guess if not ideal – umm… unfocused perhaps?), are purposefully impersonal – in that employees and customers are treated equally and dispassionately and not influenced by individual differences (okay – yes I know, this is getting a bit ridiculous now), and employment is based on technical qualifications (not awards then?).

The sick role – Talcott Parsons

Parsons??? Yes, one cannot really look at the sociological concepts in this area and escape this guy… but I have my reasons for including him…

Talcott Parsons was an American sociologist working in the early-mid 20th century who argued that being 'sick' was not just a biological condition, but a social one involving the 'sufferer' entering a social role of legitimised deviance (yep – you did read that correctly!). For Parsons, a sick person was not a fully functional and productive cog within a wider functioning social machine, but a form of deviance that needed management (by medical professionals). For Parsons, being sick brought with it certain 'obligations' to uphold in order to be afforded to benefits or 'rights' of the 'sick role'. The 'rights' the sick person were entitled to consisted of being exempt from 'normal social roles' and not being held responsible for their medical condition. In order to meet these rights however, the sick person was obliged to 'try and get well' and to 'cooperate with the medical professional'. Parsons then went on to categorise the sick into three categories: the conditionally sick (i.e. requiring a sick note to be excused from work), the unconditionally legitimate (seen as permanently incapable of being functional productive individuals), and illegitimate (or people seen as 'malingerers').

Why do I introduce such an ableist theory you might ask? Perhaps to show the historical theoretical roots of the rationalisation of those classed as sick and disabled. Of course, there are many criticisms made of this theory, patients may not be erm... 'patient', those under such management may resist dependency on medical expertise, doctors may not be as perfect in their prescriptions as Parsons may have hoped for. Also, how does one assess and treat someone, who is umm... not 'ill' in the first place? Despite the obvious flaws in this theory, it has certainly been part of a legacy of justifications for the power of medical expertise over that of the (sometimes not so) 'patient'.

The mortification of self – Erving Goffman

A list of sociological concepts would not ever feel right to me without this guy being included...

Erving Goffman was a sociologist who began publishing his work in the 1950s. His work covered many fascinating areas of study, from impression management to stigma. I often wondered how someone in an elevated position deals with their impression management when they have been found to hold a discrediting stigma, such as presiding over numerous failed inspections, but I digress...

It is Goffman's seminal work on asylums and what he called 'total institutions' that I want to draw attention, and its adjoining concept of the 'mortification of self'. A total institution is one that has been rationally developed to house the socially taboo and stigmatised, where the 'inmates' live their entire lives under institutional rules, and where they attempt to close themselves off from the attention of the outside world, such as prisons, concentration camps, and mental asylums. It is quite clear that ATUs fit this category only too well.

For Goffman, total institutions were 'experiments in what could be done to the self', where the 'inmates' went through a process of 'mortification of self'. This concept refers to how the individual identities of those living within total institutions are stripped away. The more degraded and institutionalised they become, the more they are subjected to conditions which remove identity markers, from being called by one's surname at a boarding school, to having to wear a designated uniform, the tactics are many. Such treatment creates a separation between the 'inmates' previous sense of self and their new institutionalised sense of self, where an individual is not allowed private space, or even a self which one can manage the impression of.

When one looks at the inhuman treatment that often occurs in ATUs, one needs to look beyond individual psychological explanations of conduct and analyse the way that such 'treatment' is socially organised.

Fatalistic suicide – Emile Durkheim

Why do I bring up something like suicide in relation to the theme of ATUs? This is because of a framework proposed by Emile Durkheim in the late 19th century (another of those 'founding fathers' of sociology). Durkheim contended that incidences of suicide were dependent on social circumstances. He suggested that within the fragmenting societies of the then 'modern era', that suicide rates would rise due to increasing social isolation and a lack of moral regulation of its members (something those wishing to understand why in a recent study in Sweden it was found that autistic people without additional learning difficulties were nine times as likely to commit suicide than the average may wish to look into perhaps?). Durkheim also hypothesised that there would be an increase in what he called 'fatalistic suicide' within social conditions where a person encounters extreme oppression and excessive regulation of their lives, having their interests and passions suffocated. Durkheim hypothesised that for some, for example prisoners or slaves, they may find themselves in such a fatalistic situation, that the only perceived route of escape is that of suicide.

Durkheim did not have much in the way of evidence to support this claim, yet the idea of what was to happen to a human being when their autonomy was stripped away (such as in the process of the 'mortification of self') was to be again theorised in the 1960s, this time by a psychologist by the name of Martin Seligman in the theory of 'learned helplessness' (yes, I know I am cheating here by introducing a psychological concept, but it is relevant to the idea of fatalism within a social situation...). Yes, as my friend and colleague Andy McDonnell likes to point out, Seligman – the champion of positive psychology – started out experimenting with electric shocks through floor plates to subject an animal (dogs) to inescapable aversive stimuli to see how they would react! What Seligman found in these experiments were that the dogs would eventually stop trying to avoid the stimulus and behave as if utterly helpless to change the situation. Even when opportunities to escape were presented anew, the dogs had learned to feel helpless and did not act.

Whilst humans may react quite differently to dogs, it is not difficult to imagine a hopeless situation where one has no control over the outcome, and how this might affect how one acts (or not). Such a feeling of helplessness has been linked to depression and anxiety.

Autistic people have often commented that when under extreme stress, they can exhaust themselves, 'burnout', and 'shut down'. In rare cases, it has been known for people to enter a catatonic state, although this has can also be linked as a potential reaction to antipsychotic medication. When one looks at the stories emerging from #7Daysofaction, it would suggest that extreme measures of prone restraint, overmedication, and creating barriers to family contact are commonplace. Of course, autistic people can be stubborn, resistant, and persistent, and may not understand fully what is happening to them, and thus way well rebel (often leading to ever more constraining practices). Yet, even the strongest of wills can be damaged, sometimes beyond repair. Such rationalising of extreme measures can only originate from seeing the people in one's 'care' being treated as 'other', as not fully human.

The other – Simone de Beauvoir

One of the primary influences on what is often referred to as the 'second wave' of feminism was the seminal work *The Second Sex* written by Simone de Beauvoir and published in 1949. In this book, she argued that men had traditionally seen themselves as complete or in reference to other men, with women being seen as a deviation from this central power, the 'other'. Whilst one could argue to what extent this centrality has shifted or not, little could perhaps compare to the extreme othering that occurs within total institutions. The abuses documented in #7Daysofaction could not be possible without the mortification of self process and a level of othering to a level of being dehumanised.

Relating this concept again to psychology, an important contribution to this area was made by Henri Tajfel and colleagues in their work regarding 'social identity theory'. In this theory, a social identity is the sense of who a person is when related to group memberships, which can be self-identifications or imposed upon people (sometimes with very negative consequences – see Goffman again – this time on his notions of stigma). For Tajfel, the groups people perceive that they belonged to were at the same time, a source of pride and belonging, but also gave rise to discriminating against those seen as part of an 'out-group', especially if such a group is set up in opposition to one's own in terms of its defining features. This can produce difficulties in all walks of life – just think of what a negative spiral can ensue when a teacher moans negatively about their students and vice-versa. If one sees others purely by their role and build an oppositional culture, battles will be the end product. Often it is the 'inmates' (and their loved ones) who are classified as 'oppositional' by the (ir)rationalised view of those running total institutions, and in the case of the battles that rage within and outside ATUs, they can become further reasoning for incarceration.

An essential part of Tajfel's theory is categorisation, thus when someone is categorised as essentially 'other' and not like oneself, this becomes an excuse for all kinds of abuses. Tajfel also suggested that such actions can be legitimised by reference to group norms – or the attempt at them anyway (need I reference the line 'we are not an outlier'?).

Iatrogenesis – Ivan Illich

And so I get to the concept that gave me the idea for this essay. Iatrogenesis is a term that originates in the Greek term for 'brought forth by the healer' and is used to refer to when a person is adversely affected by the actions of medical practitioners. The mid-20th century theorist Ivan Illich utilised this term and broadened it to a framework of three kinds. Firstly – clinical iatrogenesis, where direct injury is patients due to ineffective, unsafe, and erroneous treatments and practices, you know – like when people are regularly subjected to prone restraint, overmedicated, or die whilst unsupervised and taking a bath. The second aspect Illich talked about was that of 'social iatrogenesis', which referred to the ever-increasing medicalisation of life, so more of our lives become under the rationalised direction of medical professionals and companies. Lastly, Illich talked of 'cultural iatrogenesis', where traditional ways of coping with life were removed from people to be replaced by rationalised medical prescriptions. For Illich, through this process, people can lose their own autonomous coping skills and strategies. Under the processes of the mortification of self within ATUs, such autonomous skills may fall away, whilst 'coping strategies' such as self-harming increase.

Interactional expertise – Harry Collins and Rob Evans

The last concept I want to explore is that of 'interactional expertise' developed by contemporary theorists Harry Collins and Rob Evans. Collins and Evans produced a classification of how people come to acquire expertise and tacit knowledge. Whilst the 'contributory experts' regarding what it is like to be autistic or have learning disabilities, or be a family member of someone placed in an ATU, are the people themselves, 'interactional expertise' is when one is able to communicate the practice language of contributory experts. So, by reading this essay, you may have gained a small amount of expertise in being able to talk the talk of a sociologist, although (unless you are one) you would probably not be able to 'pass' as a sociologist from such limited information alone. As I have argued in academic papers myself – the interactional expertise even so-called experts in the field of autism can have with autistic people can leave something to be desired. Given what I have previously called the 'double empathy problem' (simplistically – that both autistic and non-autistic people can struggle to empathise with one another) between people of differing dispositions however, this is perhaps to be expected. Yet if one were to be looking to better the welfare and well-being of autistic people, people with learning disabilities, and family members, perhaps learning from these 'contributory experts' would be a good starting point (you'd think!). Instead, we have a situation where people are subjected to life in a total institution, rationally designed to mortify their self-identities and replace them with institutionally prescribed roles – leading to othering and depersonalisation (of staff too), an 'us and them' mentality, and people becoming worse off than they were to begin with (thus triggering more tools of surveillance and control – yes – oh and I got this far without mentioning Foucault…).

What if things were different?

When looking at social relations, however 'reified' (oh – there I go again – okay – made to seem natural and real when something is socially created by people – or 'clumped') they become, one can change social structures and relations (or 'unblock the clump').

What if the support and care of autistic people and those with learning disabilities were not organised by large-scale bureaucracies?

What if those commissioning services were autistic people, people with learning disabilities, and their families (the contributory experts)?

How can one hold degraded and dysfunctional bureaucracies to account if they are allowed to continue failing?

If autistic people and people with learning disabilities are not 'ill' and normativity is a moving target and not an ideal, than autistic people and those with learning disabilities are not 'deviant' either (although no doubt would be to Parsons) – so what is being controlled? A social taboo?

What if one reversed the mortification of self – what would that look like? Empowerment of self-identity? What structures could help in this regard?

An empowered life would not be a fatalistic one without a future to be imagined. An empowered life means not being seen as 'other'. As the autistic activist Jim Sinclair once said:

> *'Grant me the dignity of meeting me on my own terms.'*

It also doesn't mean doing the opposite and providing no support at all. If such 'care in the community' is to work, it means commitment and a transfer of funds away from ATUs.

What would social supports look like if not premised on a medicalised account of disability? This essay may seem like I am simply 'bashing' medical professionals – this is not my intent. My intent is for people to analyse what is happening and to think of alternatives. Having said that, most of these concepts are getting quite old now, perhaps it is time those rationalising services 'learnt lessons'?

In the spirit of action though, we better finish with the words of Karl Marx (the last of those 'founding fathers' of sociology):

> *'Philosophers have merely interpreted the world in various ways, the point is to change it.'*

Part 4: Participation

The final section of this collection concentrates on another main thread that has run through my work, and that is the topic of participation. For too long the autistic voice has been frozen out of the research process, other than being the passive recipients of a largely medical gaze. The first chapter in this section directly addresses this point and was written with my colleague Dr Mike Bracher. The second chapter was written as part of the '107 days' and 'Justice for LB' campaigns and dedicated to the memory of Connor Sparrowhawk (aka 'Laughing Boy'). This case highlighted the opposite of meaningful participation for both Connor and his family and is a devastating indictment of how eroded 'care and support' can become for autistic people and those with learning disabilities. The third chapter in this section reflects on the concept of the 'Aut-ethnography'. While the method of 'auto-ethnography' appealed to me, the notion of constructing a coherent narrative of self over time did not. This essay explores how an autistic narrative of self might be constructed. The fourth chapter in this collection is a research article written with my colleague Dr Tara Sims. This piece of research analysed the narratives found in *Asperger United* magazine and particularly concentrated on issues of well-being and belonging. The themes that came out of this research highlighted the social alienation and isolation often suffered by autistic people, and the need for recognition and meaningful social connections. The final chapter in this collection summarises my PhD thesis, which looked into the educational ideology and practices of various stakeholders in regard to the education of secondary school aged autistic children. The full thesis is available free online from the University of Birmingham library.

I am at present working on new projects such as the 'Participatory Autism Research Collective' (PARC) (see www.PARCautism.co.uk) and the 'Shaping Autism Research UK' seminar series. These initiatives are building on and promoting participatory frameworks. However, given the findings of the 'Future Shaped Together' report (Pellicano *et al* 2013), there is much work to be done if the sparseness of participatory (or even social) research in the field of autism studies is to be addressed.

Reference

Pellicano L, Dinsmore A & Charman T (2013) *A Future Shaped Together: Shaping autism research in the UK.* London: Institute of Education.

Autistics speak but are they heard?

By Damian E M Milton and Mike Bracher

This article was first published in Medical Sociology Online **7**(2) *61–69, in 2013.*

Abstract

In this article, we argue that the exclusion of autistic people from meaningful involvement in research is both ethically and epistemologically problematic, and constitutes a significant barrier to research impact. By the term 'meaningful', we refer to the inclusion of different autistic voices not merely as sources of empirical material, but as active participants in the production of knowledge on autism. We discuss two trends in research that are of concern: firstly, the failure to explore and engage fully with the lived experiences of participants in social research; secondly, imposition of problematic narratives on autistic experiences, linked to partial or complete absence of engagement with the diverse work of autistic authors. We conclude by pointing to some contemporary developments and intellectual exchanges that serve as exemplars which increase the ethical and epistemological integrity of research on the lived experiences of autistic people.

Introduction

The majority of published research in autism has emerged from areas allied to clinical practice; a consequence of which has been an almost exclusive focus on the condition as involving only deficits. While there are indications (Baron-Cohen *et al*, 2009; Mottron *et al*, 2006), that this is beginning to change – and that an appreciation of autism as involving a range of potential strengths and limitations is emerging – the view that still dominates mainstream research is that of autism as consisting exclusively of deficit. This has a range of implications: one of which is the exclusion of autistic voices from processes of knowledge production. We argue that this produces ethical and epistemological problems that are interrelated, such as the tendency to pathologise behaviours that may be seen as 'bizarre' or 'strange' to the observer without exploring their subjective rationale. In addition, there is also a lack of exploration of variation and contingency in the lives of autistic people (in particular adults), which stifles the development of more ecologically grounded understandings of autistic people's lives. However, some emerging developments in research participation may help overcome these limitations, and these are discussed in the final section of the paper.

Framing autism

Autism spectrum conditions are commonly understood as involving difficulties in social communication, social interaction, and social imagination (Baron-Cohen, 2008; NAS, 2011). Social communication difficulties can include problems with facial expressions and body language, or with conveying implicit meaning in written or spoken language (Baron-Cohen, 2008: 58). Many autistic people also experience the world differently from non-autistic people, in terms of their sensory and perceptual experiences of, for example, light levels or patterns, sounds, particular smells, colours, textures or tastes (Bogdashina, 2003: 44–83). This can affect the quality and/or intensity of what is experienced, resulting in hyper / hyposensitivities (i.e. a more or less intense experience of stimuli than the range typical in non-AS people), that tend to be multimodal (i.e. taking different experiential forms and occurring in different sense domains) and pervasive) (Kern *et al*, 2006; Klintwall *et al*, 2011; Leekam *et al*, 2007; Samson *et al*, 2011; Tomchek & Dunn, 2007).

How autism manifests can vary significantly between individuals and this is socially mediated, via a process of constant interaction with changing environments. For example, even within a setting where an annoying sound is present, a person may be able to persevere in their intended actions, if the social environment is conducive and/or their awareness is directed significantly away from the noise (Bogdashina, 2001, 4-7). However, if the social context and/or environment presents other issues, perhaps sensory (for example, too many sounds or lights) or social (for example, anxiety in the presence of unfamiliar company) then this can affect a person's threshold of tolerance (Bogdashina, 2001, 4-7).

While problems with social and environmental aspects of the everyday world are common features of life for people on the spectrum, 'being autistic' should not be framed purely through a deficit model lens (Baron-Cohen *et al*, 2009; Gernsbacher et *al*, 2006; Milton, 2012). Indeed, there is evidence that autistics routinely outperform non-autistics in a range of perceptual, reasoning and comprehension tasks. However, these appear less likely to be reported, or are reported as further evidence of deficit rather than an associated strength (Dawson *et al*, 2007; Gernsbacher *et al*, 2006). Conversely, for many people, autistic experiences are central to their well-being and sense of self, and social and cultural constraints mediate the extent to which they can freely experience these ways of being (Gernsbacher *et al*, 2006; Milton & Moon, 2012a; Milton, 2012). This is not to argue that AS related differences are reducible to either social or cultural factors; rather to emphasise that individual experiences of 'being AS' are inextricably linked to the conditions in which lives are lived (Molloy & Vasil, 2004).

Despite evidence in the autistic population of a range of neurodevelopmental differences when they are compared with non-autistics (Schroeder *et al*, 2010), autism remains a condition that is defined and diagnosed through observation.

There exists no definitive account of its development, and current research points away from a single 'cause' towards a range of potential neurodevelopmental differences (Happe *et al*, 2006) – to say nothing of variations in social and cultural circumstances in which autistic people live. Hacking (1999) frames autism in terms of an interface between biology and culture, where factors relating to each domain are necessary but not sufficient to explain or even define observed differences between autistic and non-autistic people. Further, he argues that, in autism, biological factors appear to interact with classifications through social processes, giving rise to what he terms an 'interactive' phenomenon (Hacking, 1999). Classifying an object as a table does not change anything about its material properties (Hacking refers to this as a 'flat effect' that is unchanging). However, classifying human beings can alter both the conceptual and material conditions of what is observed, which can then, in turn, affect classifications, through what Hacking (1999) terms a 'looping effect'. For example, he observes that variations in institutional and interactive responses to those classified as 'autistic' can change the context in which features identified with autism may arise (Hacking, 1999). Setting up AS as a generalised deficit in sociality, for example, may frame social encounters with people categorised in such a way that breaches in interactions become more visible or more likely (e.g. in programs of therapy, support services, or changes to educational, study and workplace environments).

Exclusion and marginalisation of autistic voices – historical and contemporary examples

Given these conditions, distributions of power and opportunities to speak in the process of knowledge production on autism matter very much in terms of how it is understood, and how autistic people are seen and treated by non-autistic others.

> '...right from the start, from the time someone came up with the word 'autism', the condition has been judged from the outside, by its appearances, and not from the inside according to how it is experienced'. (Williams, 1996: 14)

Talking about autism was, for many years after its emergence in the work of Leo Kanner (Feinstein, 2010; Grinker, 2008), the exclusive preserve of clinicians and researchers, where autistic people were objects of inspection, rather than active participants in the creation of knowledge relating to their own experiences. While the emergence of self-advocacy movements and the entrance of academically trained autistic researchers into knowledge production has begun to challenge these conditions (for example: Arnold, 2010; Dawson *et al*, 2007; Graby, 2012; Milton, 2012; Murray *et al*, 2005), these tend to be the exception.

Obtaining the views of disabled people is now a requirement of policy legislation, both nationally and internationally (Pellicano & Stears, 2011; UN, 2006). Yet this remains tokenistic when policies and research concerning people with a particular disability fail to include them in a meaningful way in agenda setting in both research and service provision. Such a situation is reflected in the lack of involvement and representation that autistic people have in organisations with stated aims that include the support of autistic people (Milton *et al*, 2012). In particular, the experiences and needs of autistic adults are often poorly understood by service providers, and the experiences of adults are under-researched (Allard, 2009; Rosenblatt, 2008). Financial pressures may, of course, play a role in this, as Ne'eman observes:

> 'Of over $314 million in research funding, only 3% went to research into services, support and education and less than 1% went to research into the needs of adults.' (Ne'eman, 2011)

Consequently, research does not address the conflict between the groundswell of autistic voices and efforts of self-advocacy, on the one hand, and those espousing a discourse of deficiency and dependency on the other (Milton *et al*, 2012). Although many within the autistic community have adopted the political slogan of: 'Nothing about us, without us' (for example, the Autistic Self-Advocacy Network (ASAN)), research in autism continues to silence autistic voices within knowledge production, also side-lining potential valuable insights from research that engages with lived experiences. Failure to acknowledge and explore the different personal and social conditions in which autistic people live and implications for their well-being is therefore a significant barrier to impact in contemporary research.

The answer does not lie simply in funding research that engages with lived experience (although this is undoubtedly an important issue), but there is a need to explore how autistic people can be involved as participants in the processes of knowledge production. All too often, autistic participant contributions to social research are quarantined beneath what we refer to as a 'glass subheading', treated only as empirical material for inspection and analysis by non-autistic researchers, and thus opportunities for mutual reflection and exploration are missed. This is significant because it means that understandings of well-being – what makes life liveable and everyday worlds inhabitable for different autistic people – are framed by third-person observers. For example, Jennes-Coussens *et al* (2006) explored the quality of life of 12 young AS men aged 18–21 through measures based upon the World Health Organisation's Quality of Life measure, with little discussion of how these factors might play out within the lives of specific participants. The authors claim at one point that 'results [relating to satisfaction with physical health] may relate to clumsiness of movements or to sensory hypersensitivity' (Jennes-Coussens *et al*, 2006: 410). However, they do not appear to have followed up on this point with participants in their semi-structured interviews, limiting the specificity and scope of this claim. In Lawrence *et al*'s (2010) investigation of the transition to adulthood, the authors' use of Maslow's hierarchy of needs to frame important areas limits their engagement with first person narratives in their review of literature. While they emphasise 'self-actualisation' as important for maintaining quality of life, they give no examples of how this might be achieved by specific people, nor do they discuss what this might mean for different autistic people in different contexts. Elsewhere, Portway and Johnson (2005) explored the 'risks of a non-obvious disability' for adults diagnosed with Asperger Syndrome. Here the unqualified description of the behaviours of their participants as 'odd' or 'bizarre' means that they neglect to explore the potential meaning or significance of these activities as legitimate and valued experiences, or as important strategies for coping with social and/or sensory issues (2005: 80).

The failure to engage fully with first-person experiences in exploring the lives of autistic people is both ethically and epistemologically significant in the context of contemporary research, because well-being does not simply mean the absence of difficulty, but also the ability for individuals to be involved in their communities, and to pursue happiness, as underscored by the World Health Organisation's (WHO) definition of 'mental health':

> 'Mental health is defined as a state of well-being in which every individual realizes his or her own potential, can cope with the normal stresses of life, can work productively and fruitfully, and is able to make a contribution to her or his community.' (WHO, 2014).

In the case of autistic people, well-being also relates to a person's ability to experience ways of being that are compatible with their dispositions, without being forced to mimic non-autistic behaviours that can be confusing or bewildering to them (Bogdashina, 2001; Milton, 2012). It is known that autistic people – in particular adults – suffer high levels of social isolation, unemployment, and economic difficulties, as well as physical and mental ill health, and that this is attended by variable and often poor understanding of their needs (Allard, 2009; Rosenblatt, 2008). Therefore, it is crucial that researchers explore the subjective significance of AS related experiences in relation to well-being, as this may not be immediately apparent to non-AS observers.

Imposing narratives – ethical and epistemological consequences of dis/engagement with autistic authors

Another worrying aspect of some academic publications that are positioned within or draw on theoretical and methodological resources from social science, is the imposition of narratives that produce a distorted picture of life experience - in part due to a failure to engage with the writings of autistic people. In their book *The Myth of Autism*, Timimi *et al* (2010) argue that the changing history of the autism spectrum, and failure to provide clear etiological explanations indicates that the diagnostic label is of no scientific, clinical or social value, and should therefore be abolished. They claim that this would be a desirable outcome for those currently diagnosed as being on the spectrum – a bold step for which they provide worryingly little evidence or discussion in terms of concrete ethical implications

(Bracher & Thackray, 2012). More troubling in the context of the present discussion, however, is the authors' failure to engage with a diversity of accounts of experience from autistic people themselves. This is problematic not only in epistemological terms, but also ethically. Much of the existing writing from autistic authors is critical of current diagnostic categories; something which casts further doubt on the ethical and intellectual integrity of many contemporary arguments.

Where autistic voices have been integrated into discussions by non-autistic academics, these tend to involve problematic interpretations of the source material, an example of which comes from Ruud Hendricks' (2012) *Autistic Company*. In this book, Hendriks explores how autistic and non-autistic people navigate a shared existence, and considers how one can talk about the unusual forms of interaction that take place (Hendriks, 2012). In so doing, the author approaches a topic not only of paramount importance within the field of autism studies, but also medical sociology more generally, in terms of how to build interactions and relationships with neurodiverse populations (Hendriks, 2012). His main focus is on the forms of living that autistic and non-autistic people establish together, and he suggests that the metaphors commonly used to describe autistic people underestimate commonalities; that dispositional differences are not irreconcilable extremes (Hendriks, 2012). Here, the reason for autistic people being outsiders in society is formulated as a lack of insight in context-related meaning. Hendricks concludes that a shared existence is dependent on the widening of companionship to include physical as well as mental connections (Hendriks, 2012). However, Hendriks' selective engagement with the works of autistic authors leads to some highly questionable suggestions. For example, he suggests that a stimulus-free and controlling environment is the only way to help autistic people connect with others, and that 'leaving autistic people alone' will lead to them becoming lost in the world (Hendriks, 2012). This reifies behaviourist modification techniques to stimulate 'normal development' and reduce 'autistic behaviour' - techniques that are highly criticised by some autistic self-advocates (Dawson, 2004; Milton & Moon, 2012b). While one would not recommend neglect for any child, building reciprocity requires mutuality of understanding rather than the onesided imposition that Hendricks appears to advocate. As Ryan and Räisänen (2008) have observed, autistics are often very aware of the conditions of life 'over there' in the non-autistic world; and in a way that is not often reciprocated. Elsewhere, Ochs and Solomon (2010) have indicated that adjustments in dispositional alignments in parent / child interactions can help to alleviate some of the difficulties inherent in autistic/non-autistic interactions.

Hendriks asks how to prevent a non-autistic interpretation from 'gaining the upper hand after all' (Hendriks, 2012: 149). Co-researching and co-writing with an autistic writer or scholar might provide a useful starting point. If interactional expertise is to be gained, it is essential that normative assumptions and impositions of non-autistic meanings are deconstructed. Instead, Hendriks' examination of autistic autobiographies ends up being an exercise in 'quote-mining' to fit the claims being made; claims that are often critiqued by some of the authors cited by Hendriks (such as Sinclair & Baggs) (Hendriks, 2012: 18-19: 149-150: 178). Despite seeking to position his research in the disability studies literature (Arnold, 2010; Goodley, 2011; Meekosha *et al*, 2013), Hendriks is not attuned to the anti-normative stance that characterises this body of work and end up working against the activist rallying cry of 'nothing about us, without us'. Indeed, if Hendrik's conceptualisations were valid, the social awareness required in order to enable collaboration between the autistic and non-autistic authors of the current paper could not have been achieved.

Possible alternatives

Despite the prevalence of exclusion in contemporary research, examples of good practice do exist, such as the *Autism Asperger Partnership in Research and Education (AASPIRE)* – a group that carries out research projects in collaboration with academic communities, 'relevant to the needs of adults on the spectrum' (Nicolaidis *et al*, 2011; Nicolaidis *et al*, 2012). This group advocates the use of 'community based participatory research' or 'participatory action research', where autistic people engage as equal partners throughout the research process (Nicolaidis *et al*., 2011; Nicolaidis *et al*., 2012). Some of the principles of this style of research are: to build on the strengths and resources of the community; to facilitate co-learning and 'capacity' building between participant; and to disseminate results to all partners. Parallel aspirations have been expressed by the autistic community in Britain: for example, the 'Autscape' conference in 2011 included a presentation concerning the 'owning' of autism research, providing advice with regard to how research is carried out and highlighting challenges to address when considering participation (Autscape, 2011; Kalen, 2011). More recently, an autistic run academic journal (Autonomy, 2013) has been established, and a project – entitled 'Theorising Autism' (Milton & Moon, 2012b) – has been set up with the aim of bringing autistic academics together, in order to bolster collaborative efforts. Meanwhile the agenda of the majority of autism research continues to be dominated by concerns relating to finding a 'cause', normalisation through behavioural modification, and 'hopes of a cure' – wrapped in a rhetoric of 'scientifically supportable evidence-based practice' (Post *et al* 2012). In order for there to be a significant shift in the research agenda, the silencing of autistic voices and tokenistic practices must be replaced by meaningful involvement of autistic people in understanding autism – including (but not limited to) the employment of appropriately trained autistic people in research teams. With such involvement, the research agenda would be broadened, rapport with research participants might improve, dissemination of findings would be less offensive to the autistic community, and autistic people would be less alienated from knowledge produced in the field. Crucially, such developments would increase the epistemological integrity of studies that seek to explore important questions relating to the well-being of autistic people.

Authors' note – both authors contributed equally to the production of this paper.

References

Allard A (2009) Transition to Adulthood: Inquiry into transition to adulthood for young people with autism. London: The National Autistic Society & The All-Party Parliamentary Group on Autism.

Arnold L (2010) *The Medium is the Message: Autism, Ethics and Society.* London: UCL.

Autonomy (2013) Autonomy, the *Critical Journal of Interdisciplinary Autism Studies.*

Autscape (2011) Autscape and Autism Politics.

Baron-Cohen S (2008) *Autism and Asperger Syndrome.* Oxford: Oxford University Press.

Baron-Cohen S, Ashwin E, Ashwin C, Tavassoli T & Chakrabarti B (2009) Talent in autism: hyper-systemizing, hyper-attention to detail and sensory hypersensitivity, *Philosophical Transactions of the Royal Society B: Biological Sciences* **364** 1377–1383.

Bogdashina O (2001) *A Reconstruction of the Sensory World of Autism.* Sheffield: Sheffield Hallam University Press.

Bogdashina O (2003) *Sensory Perceptual Issues in Autism and Asperger Syndrome: Different sensory experiences – different perceptual world*s. London: Jessica Kingsley.

Bracher M & Thackray L (2012) A History of Autism: Conversations with the Pioneers; Understanding Autism: Patients, Doctors, and the History of a Disorder; The Myth of Autism. *Sociology of Health & Illness* **34** (7) 1119–1122.

Dawson M (2004) *The Misbehaviour of Behaviourists: Ethical challenges to the autism-ABA industry* [online]. Available at: http://www.sentex.net/~nexus23/naa_aba.html (accessed September 2017).

Dawson M, Soulières I, Ann Gernsbacher M & Mottron L (2007) The Level and Nature of Autistic Intelligence. *Psychological Science* **18** (8) 657–662.

Feinstein A (2010) *A History of Autism: Conversations with the pioneers.* Oxford: Wiley-Blackwell.

Gernsbacher MA, Dawson M & Mottron L (2006) Autism: Common, heritable, but not harmful. *Behavioral and Brain Sciences* **29** (4).

Goodley D (2011) *Disability Studies: An interdisciplinary introduction.* Los Angeles: SAGE.

Graby S (2012) To be or not to be disabled: autism, disablement and identity politics. *Theorising Normalcy*: University of Chester.

Grinker RR (2008) *Unstrange Minds: A father remaps the world of autism*. Thriplow: Icon.

Hacking I (1999) *The Social Construction of What?* Cambridge, Mass: Harvard University Press.

Happe F, Ronald A & Plomin R (2006) Time to give up on a single explanation for autism. *Nat Neurosci* **9** (10) 1218–20.

Hendriks R (2012) *Autistic Company*. Rodopi Bv Editions.

Jennes-Coussens M, Magill-Evans J & Koning C (2006) The quality of life of young men with Asperger syndrome. *Autism* **10** (4) 403–414.

Kalen (2011) Owning autism research. *Autscape* 2011.

Kern JK, Trivedi MH, Garver CR, Grannemann BD, Andrews AA, Savla JS, Johnson DG, Mehta JA & Schroeder JL (2006) The pattern of sensory processing abnormalities in autism. *Autism* **10** (5) 480–494.

Klintwall L, Holm A, Eriksson M, Carlsson LH, Olsson MB, Hedvall Å, Gillberg C & Fernell E (2011) Sensory abnormalities in autism: A brief report. *Research in Developmental Disabilities* **32** (2) 795–800.

Leekam S, Nieto C, Libby S, Wing L & Gould J (2007) Describing the Sensory Abnormalities of Children and Adults with Autism. *Journal of Autism and Developmental Disorders* **37** (5) 894–910.

Meekosha H, Shuttleworth R & Soldatic K (2013) Disability and Critical Sociology: Expanding the Boundaries of Critical Social Inquiry. *Critical Sociology* **39** (3) 319–323.

Milton D, Mills R & Pellicano L (2012) Ethics and autism: where is the autistic voice? Commentary on Post et al. *Journal of Autism and Developmental Disorders* **44** (10).

Milton D & Moon L (2012a) 'And that, Damian, is what I call life- changing': findings from an action research project involving autistic adults in an on-line sociology study group. *Good Autism Practice* **13** (2) 32–39.

Milton D & Moon L (2012b) The normalisation agenda and the psycho-emotional disablement of autistic people. *Autonomy* **1** (1).

Milton D (2012) On the ontological status of autism: the 'double empathy problem', *Disability & Society*. **27** (6) 883–887.

Molloy H & Vasil L (2004) *Asperger Syndrome, Adolescence, and Identity: Looking beyond the label*. London: Jessica Kingsley.

Mottron L, Dawson M, Soulières I, Hubert B & Burack J (2006) Enhanced perceptual functioning in autism: an update and eight principles of autistic perception. *Journal of Autism and Developmental Disorders*. **36** (1) 27–43.

Murray D, Lesser M & Lawson W (2005) Attention, monotropism and the diagnostic criteria for autism. *Autism* **9** (2) 139–156.

NAS (2011) *Autism and Asperger Syndrome: An introduction*. London: National Autistic Society.

Ne'eman A (2011) Talk about Autism – Ari Ne'eman – 1 June 2011, London: Ambitious About Autism.

Nicolaidis C, Raymaker D, McDonald K, Dern S, Ashkenazy E, Boisclair C, Robertson S & Baggs A (2011) Collaboration strategies in nontraditional communitybased participatory research partnerships: lessons from an academic-community partnership with autistic self-advocates. *Progress in Community Health Partnerships* **5** (2) 143–50.

Nicolaidis C, Raymaker D, McDonald K, Dern S, Boisclair WC, Ashkenazy E & Baggs A (2012) Comparison of healthcare experiences in autistic and non-autistic adults: a cross-sectional online survey facilitated by an academic-community partnership. *Journal of General Internal Medicine* **28** (6).

Ochs E & Solomon O (2010) Autistic Sociality. *Ethos* **38** (1) 69–92.

Pellicano E & Stears M (2011) Bridging autism, science and society: moving toward an ethically informed approach to autism research. *Autism Research* **4** (4) 271–282.

Portway SM & Johnson B (2005) Do you know I have Asperger's syndrome? Risks of a non-obvious disability. *Health, Risk & Society* **7** (1) 73–83.

Rosenblatt M (2008) *I Exist: The message from adults with autism in England*. London: National Autistic Society.

Ryan S & Räisänen U (2008) 'It's like you are just a spectator in this thing': Experiencing social life the 'aspie' way. *Emotion, Space and Society* **1** (2) 135–143.

Samson F, Mottron L, Soulières I & Zeffiro TA (2011) Enhanced visual functioning in autism: an ALE meta-analysis. *Human Brain Mapping* **33** (7).

Schroeder JH, Desrocher M, Bebko JM & Cappadocia MC (2010) The neurobiology of autism: theoretical applications. *Research in Autism Spectrum Disorders* **4** (4) 555–564.

Timimi S, Gardner N & McCabe B (2011) *The Myth of Autism: Medicalising men's social and emotional competence*. Basingstoke: Palgrave Macmillan.

Tomchek SD & Dunn W (2007) Sensory processing in children with and without autism: a comparative study using the short sensory profile. *The American Journal of Occupational Therapy* **61** (2) 190–200.

UN (2006) *United Nations Convention on the Rights of Persons with Disabilities CRPD/C*. New York: United Nations.

WHO (2014) *Mental Health: A state of well-being* [online]. Available at: http://www.who.int/features/factfiles/mental_health/en/ (accessed September 2017).

Williams D (1996) *Autism: An inside-out approach: An innovative look at the mechanics of 'autism' and its developmental 'cousins*. London: Jessica Kingsley.

Moments in time

This article was published online as part of the #JusticeforLB and #107days campaigns in 2014.

> *'Today is World Autism Awareness Day #WAAD14 and we were delighted that Damian Milton offered to adopt the day and share his thoughts. They are as follows, it's a long but thought provoking post, worth reading every word.'*

Today, 2nd April 2014, there are many people around the world trying to raise awareness for autism, with this date each year marking World Autism Awareness Day. There are many differing ways of raising awareness of a cultural phenomenon; some do so in a way that is not so useful for autistic people. This is perhaps why today many autistic activists will be celebrating 'acceptance' of autistic people instead. What I would like to draw the World's attention to today however, are the campaigns of #JusticeforLB and #107days. On 19 March 2013, Connor Sparrowhawk (aka LB) was admitted to Slade House, an NHS assessment and treatment unit. 107 days later he died, having had a seizure whilst left unsupervised in a bath.

Around the world today, autistic people and especially those who are less verbal or are deemed 'learning disabled' are dehumanised, incarcerated, restrained, bullied, therapised, normalised, neglected, and I could carry on and on with such a list. What leads to this abuse of those divergent from the normative ideal? What leads to 'death by indifference'? How is one meant to find justice for LB and all the young (and older) 'dudes' (of whatever gender orientation)? This is something I (and many others) would like the world to think about today, the 14th day of the #107days campaign.

A step back in time

I was diagnosed as being on the autism spectrum in 2009 soon after being made redundant from a post in a further education college as a sociology lecturer. This had been the first full-time professional job I had ever managed to attain, through quite some effort after my son had been born. In 2005 my son was diagnosed as autistic with severe learning disabilities. I had myself avoided the psychiatric profession for many years prior to that, but that is another story. By 2010 however, I was completing another one of my University qualifications (I have quite a collection now), and was settling into a part-time PhD in the education of autistic people. I went to an autism related conference for the first time and met other autistic activists that I'd only previously read about. Yet I was still unemployed, living in a downtrodden neighbourhood, and had been struggling for many years to get my voice heard about matters relating to the plight of autistic people. Often I felt manipulated or tokenised, with my attempts at being heard failing to get very far. One day I was contacted by a researcher from the University of Oxford by the name of Sara Ryan. She was filming interviews with autistic people and their families for healthtalkonline. She answered all my queries, was prepared to travel to me, and treated me with a great deal of respect. When I met her, we both talked lovingly about our respective sons. Sara's own descriptions of her 'laughing boy' (LB) did not seem all that different from the way I talked (and still do) about my son, an expert giggler if ever there was one. I felt truly listened to, that my voice was being heard and recorded with others, that people may learn something from my efforts. I was grateful for the opportunity. Since then, I have gone on to present about autism over 70 times at various events and conferences, have had a number of articles published, and have a paid job as a consultant for the National Autistic Society's 'Ask autism' project. In order for autistic people to be confident to do such things, we need our allies. I felt that Sara was one of my first in the field.

The Functionalist Credentials

As an academic, I have never been a fan of the theories, ideologies, and applications of Functionalism (or for that matter Behaviourism). Words such as: Function, Behaviour, Appropriate, Normal, Independent, Role, Responsibility, Etiquette, Outcome – have all been used to 'beat me' at some point or another, and have only increased my social alienation. They are not about autism 'acceptance', and do not raise 'awareness' of anything but ill-fated attempts to 'manage' us. League tables, tick sheets, reward charts, cartoon strips outlining preferred behaviour etcetera, have done little to help me in life. Yet, it is functional credentials which are often valued in the world of 'style over substance', where the image of an organisation or their CEO counts for more than basic needs being met. I like to subvert this game by collecting credentials myself, currently: MA, PG(Cert), BA(Hons), Dip(conv), PGCE, MifI, MBPsS. Still, perhaps it is because I am autistic that I have never earned above average UK National earnings in any year of my life thus far. Often such credentials are used as a smokescreen for poor practice. I really do not care that the CEO of Southern Health (the authority that Slade House came under) has won an award in the past, their actions leading up to and after the death of LB will not be winning any awards from those who have witnessed them. Perhaps it is actions (and not behaviours) that speak louder than words?

Odd companions

Those who are aware of my work regarding the dangers of following behaviourist practices may be surprised to find that some who support Functionalist/Behaviourist ideology are also supporting the #JusticeforLB and #107days campaigns. One perhaps would not normally find autistic activists working to raise awareness of the same campaigns as a 'Challenging Behaviour Foundation'. This possibly just goes to show the scale of the disservice that Connor (LB), Sara, and their family have endured? Yet it could also show that intent is more important than the words people use? I have spent many years promoting theories and words that to me sounded more accepting and useful: person-centred, empowerment, and autonomy; only to see such words contorted and abused in practice, reduced to jargon that when applied means the complete opposite of their original intent. There are many tensions and debates within the field of autism and elsewhere, and for good reason, although it does not take a scientist to figure out how to address the basic needs that were not met in this debacle and how that led to Connor's death.

Connor (LB) was also, for the first time in his life, subjected to dangerous restraint practices whilst in the 'care' of Slade House. These practices must end, and all support for organisations which promote such practices. That means not 'lighting it up blue' this World Autism Awareness Day, but doing anything but that (see #boycottautismspeaks for more details). If you want to raise awareness for something, make the death of Connor Sparrowhawk a 'Rosa Parks' moment for the rights of disabled people. Let us bring an end to such practices and 'death by indifference' too.

Labels, words and people

Given what I think of myself and the people I have met, I have no qualms in calling myself 'autistic'. I have always preferred 'being me', although I have often wished that others had a more accepting attitude. Where I have found acceptance, love and passion, it has inspired me. Yet words can also be used to constrain, contain, control, and condescend. Frequently words are used to place us into cages, boxes, categories, in a kind of short-hand way of thinking. Here, the intent is very much to generalise, to not bother to go in to any depth of understanding, to be 'lazy'. Being within a category often 'othered' in such ways, one can grow very tired. When younger, it often made me angry – and when such ways of thinking lead to death by indifference, my anger returns.

In interactions with others, it does not take a fast paced 'social imagination' to figure out who in one's life treats you with dignity and respect, nor when someone else is treating you as little more than a label, and an othered outsider. Autistic people may not always have the words to express it, but 'we' are often very good at expressing whose company 'we' find significant and uplifting, and whose 'we' do not. When people are viewed as a 'cluster of behaviours' in need of 'functional assessments' sometimes the blatantly obvious is missed. On entering Slade House, Connor Sparrowhawk did not receive a health assessment, or any useful plan of action regarding his epilepsy, yet if one practitioner in that institution had been able to see him as a person, they would have acted differently. Slade House would be well described by what the Sociologist Erving Goffman called a 'total institution', where all activities are managed under one 'roof'. Goffman argued that such places only put people in a worse position than they were in to begin with, where a process of the 'mortification' (or death) of self takes place. One could describe it as a form of institutionalised disablism and a systemic dehumanisation process. Connor Sparrowhawk (LB) and those who have lived in such situations have their selfhood demeaned and ignored; in the case of Connor it led to his death. Staff within such institutions become implicated in this process, given uniforms and status that demarcate them from the 'inmates' or 'inpatients'. In the case of Southern Health award winning CEO, this seems to have led to a distancing, to the point where there is complete abdication of 'responsibility' (hmm… maybe not so 'functional' after all – maybe it is just the appearance of it which counts?)

Phaedrus: *But I have been told my dear Socrates, that what a budding orator needs to know is not what is really right, but what is likely to seem right in the eyes of the mass of people who are going to pass judgement: not what is really good or fine but what will seem so; and that it is this rather than truth that produces conviction.* (Plato, The Phaedrus, translated 1973, p71)

Perhaps if quality control employed some autistic people and their families, we would get better 'inspections'. Having said that, when more rigorous inspections were carried out on Slade House it failed on all counts …umm… more 'functionalist credentials' fading fast…

Face games

An even older concept from my old friend Erving Goffman is that of 'face games' – these are the words used in interaction and communication done purely for 'keeping up appearances' or 'reputation management'. This is not something that autistic people of all varieties are particularly famed for (despite some of us doing remarkably well at it considering how tricky and painful it can be for us). For some others I have met in life, such games seem like a natural 'way of being'. In my experience such traits can be found in managers, and often the higher up in the organisation, the more capable 'face gamers' one finds. I guess this makes sense if one's business is sales, image, public relations, and so on. But if one promotes style over substance, may one be left with a management structure built of smoke and mirrors, or a house of cards that will simply collapse with the slightest breeze? It is often said that a poor ability at deception is a deficit in autistic people, yet one could say that like many other things in the field, this may be a matter of salience, positionality and perception.

If one wants to know why so few autistic people are in full-time employment, perhaps we need to look at how one gains, presents and demonstrates one's 'functional credentials'? Why is it that the 'positive about disability' 2-tick system just does not seem to work for the neurologically divergent?

A long time ago in a galaxy far, far away…

As a young boy I was not as articulate and verbose as I am now, indeed I did not write more than a paragraph of continuous prose until I was 17 years-old. Instead, I tended to write in lists and numbers, diagrams and patterns. In 1984, I still somehow managed to acquire an assisted place to a private school, mainly through my maths and verbal reasoning skills, which may have hidden how I was bottom of the class at spelling, useless at grammar, and had various other issues with 'learning' in the usually prescribed ways. One term in, I, along with my family, were involved in a multi-car road traffic accident. My mother acquired a number of permanent physical disabilities, and I severe psychological trauma. Every psychiatrist who saw me in the years ahead had their own pet theory when they observed my 'behaviour'. In the school I attended, there was no pastoral care of the individual or any consideration of me personally. Indeed, it was virtually a total institution and it valued image and style over the quality of the life of its 'pupils'.

> *'It does not appear that he is very bright and therefore lack of effort compounds the problem'* (my 'Form Master', 1987)

There is a sociological pattern here, whether it my old school or Slade House, whether someone is deemed 'high-functioning' or 'learning disabled'. When the image of the institution is lauded, and the well-being and quality of life of those living within it are turned into numbers on a tick sheet to be managed, lives are ruined and in many cases put at risk of serious harm and can lead in all too many cases to death.

So what are the intentions of Southern Health?

Epilepsy 'benchmarking', 'advanced training' in ???, deepest apologies (whilst asking to meet with 'the family')... I am not sure what #JusticeforLB will look like, but this is not it. As an autistic person, here is my message to Southern Health: look into your restraint practices and how to change them for a start. Have autistic adults train your staff about autism – you can start now. Have a collaborative culture with parents, family and friends, and do not block them out (as this would be an action one might expect from an abusive relationship).

The last thing an organisation should do in these circumstances is defend their record and try and sweep problems even further 'under the carpet', but from the outset, this seems to have been the intention of Southern Health. If there is to be a paradigm shift in the practices of Southern Health and elsewhere, maybe they need to be educated, trained, and inspected by those who have the real passion for autistic people, those with learning disabilities, and their families – i.e. autistic people, and parents such as Sara Ryan and Mark Neary?

A final request

Today, on World Autism Awareness Day, join with me in raising awareness for #JusticeforLB and #107days. Join with me in accepting autistic people as 'we' are, and work together with us to build a better quality of life for us all.

Aut-ethnography: working from the 'inside-out'

This article was first published online as a blog post for 'The Autism Anthropologist' in 2015.

> *'And you may ask yourself, well – how did I get here?'* (Talking Heads – 'Once in a Lifetime').

Many readers of this blog will be aware of how some sociological and anthropological scholars have been turning their gaze toward autistic ways of being in the world. What readers may be less aware of is that there are also a number of autistic scholars who have been working in such fields for many years, often on the margins of academia (Arnold, 2012; Milton, 2014a). One can see expressions of how autistic people have sought to inform knowledge production in the field through their lived experience since the inception of autistic self-advocacy (e.g. Sinclair, 1993), to more recent academic commentary pieces on the potential epistemological value of autistic people being fully involved throughout the research process (Milton & Bracher, 2013; Milton, 2014b).

In this article, I will be sketching a path through some of my own work in the field and how this work links in with wider efforts within the autistic community. Instead of starting at the 'beginning' in the sense of usual, coherent linear narrative, I will 'begin' in the recent past and work backwards / sideways / 'any-old-which-ways' – p.s. this is not an 'overview'.

In a recent article (Milton, 2014c) aimed primarily for an audience of psychiatrists and medical practitioners working with autistic clients, I gave an account of my own experiences with the psychiatric profession and the fragmented sense of self-identity that I have experienced. In doing so, I gave what I referred to as an 'aut-ethnography'. Unlike auto-ethnography, which often seeks to construct a coherent narrative of self over time, to me an aut-ethnography (at least my experience/version) is a fragmented one, where snippets of information are formed into 'rhizomatic' patterns of shifting meanings. Interestingly to me, Melanie Yergeau, an American autistic scholar and activist, referred to an essay she had written as an 'autie-ethnographic narrative' (Yergeau, 2013).

For me, much autistic scholarship (albeit those who have become involved in 'hard science' disciplines) has unsurprisingly argued for, and highlighted the value of, subjective lived experience in learning about what it is to be autistic (Williams, 1996; Lawson, 2010). Many autistic activists refer to the social model (or indeed post-social models) of disability and critique purely deficit model definitions of what autism 'is', whilst not wishing to detract from the huge challenges that autistic people in, all our diversity, experience in navigating social life. This 'standpoint epistemology' and arguments over the value of such knowledge can be seen as reminiscent of previous debates in social science regarding insider/outsider interpretations, Orientalism, situated knowledge, and so on.

Autism does not just represent a form of cultural understanding however (although yes – autistic communities and culture do 'exist' for anyone still not sure), but also refers to differing neurological embodiments and dispositional affordances that shape one's interactions with social life (Milton, 2014a) – one of the consequences of which being the 'double empathy problem' (Milton, 2012; 2014b; Chown, 2014).

My own theorising regarding the 'double empathy problem' came about owing to the disjuncture I felt with the dominance of 'theory of mind' or 'mentalising' theory within the field. Such theorising leads to the framing of the social interaction difficulties that autistic people face as primarily located within the brain/mind of the autistic person, rather than in a breakdown in reciprocity and communication between two differently disposed 'social actors' (Milton, 2012). According to 'double empathy' theory, it is a problem experienced by both parties, otherwise why would autistic ways of being be such an 'enigma' to non-autistic 'experts' in the field. This breakdown in understanding has been remarked upon in some form or another by many autistic writers (e.g. Yergeau, 2013) with the theory of the 'double empathy problem' attempting to situate such an understanding within sociological and social psychology theory, leaning heavily on the work of Goffman and Garfinkel amongst others.

Since this initial formulation, the theory has been expanded by other autistic scholars (Chown, 2014), and in my own work, on the acquiring of 'interactional expertise' influenced by the work of Harry Collins and Rob Evans (Milton, 2014b). The 'seed' of how I came to these ideas came from working on philosophical ideas of disposition and difference that I had been developing all my academic life, including the years before I came into contact with the concept/construction of 'autism' (Milton, 2014a). As autistic people, whether academically oriented or not, one often becomes acutely aware that one is not one of the 'in crowd' but a cultural 'outsider'. After time, some realise that their perceptions are markedly different to other peoples, but with effort one can learn systematically to at least build a level of 'interactional expertise' and, this goes for non-autistic people attempting to interact with autistic people too! On a pragmatic level, this means that one may not be able to 'walk the walk', but one may be able to gain a level of understanding of autistic 'talk' (whether verbally articulated or not).

In order to build interactive expertise in both directions, and to build bridges across the 'double empathy' divide, we need to discover ways to work together, which consequently would mean building inclusive communities of practice where autistic expertise (Milton, 2014b) is neither devalued nor tokenised (Milton & Bracher, 2013). To build trusting and practically workable partnerships, however, means establishing equal status between those working on such projects and for autistic people to no longer be stuck behind the 'glass sub-heading' (Milton & Bracher, 2013), and 'fishbowled' (Moon, cited in Milton & Moon, 2012) for the benefit of non-autistic researchers.

References

Arnold L (2012) Autism: its relationship to science and to people with the condition. *Autonomy: The Critical Journal of Interdisciplinary Autism Studies* **1** (1).

Chown N (2014) More on the ontological status of autism and double empathy. *Disability and Society* **29** (10) 1672–1676.

Lawson W (2010) *The Passionate Mind: How people with autism learn*. London: Jessica Kingsley.

Milton D (2012) On the ontological status of autism: the 'double empathy problem'. *Disability and Society* **27** (6) 883–887.

Milton (2014a) Embodied sociality and the conditioned relativism of dispositional diversity. *Autonomy: The Critical Journal of Interdisciplinary Autism Studies* **1** (3).

Milton D (2014b) Autistic expertise: a critical reflection on the production of knowledge in autism studies. *Autism* DOI:10.1177/1362361314525281.

Milton D (2014c) Becoming autistic: an aut-ethnography. Cutting Edge Psychiatry in Practice. Issue 4: *Autism Spectrum Disorder:* 185-192.

Milton D & Bracher M (2013) Autistics speak but are they heard? *Medical Sociology Online* **7** (2) 61–69.

Milton D & Moon L (2012) 'And that Damian is what I call life changing': findings from an action research project involving autistic adults in an online sociology study group. *Good Autism Practice* **13** (2) 32–39.

Sinclair J (1993) *Don't Mourn For Us* [online]. Available at: http://www.autreat.com/dont_mourn.html (accessed September 2017).

Williams D (1996) *Autism: An inside-out approach*. London: Jessica Kingsley.

Yergeau M (2013) Clinically significant disturbance: on theorists who theorize theory of mind. *Disability Studies Quarterly* **33** (4).

How is a sense of well-being and belonging constructed in the accounts of autistic adults?

By Damian EM Milton and Tara Sims

This essay is derived in part from an article published in Disability & Society on 02 Jun 2016, available online: http://wwww.tandfonline.com/ http://dx.doi.org/10.1080/09687599.2016.1186529

Abstract

This small-scale exploratory study sought to develop an understanding of the meaning of well-being and social belonging as represented within the narratives of adults on the autism spectrum. Employing an interpretivist approach facilitated the investigation of potential contributory factors to these lived experiences in order to inform further research regarding both this topic, and service provision for adults on the autism spectrum. The project involved a thematic analysis of issues of the magazine Asperger United (AU). Four broad main themes were identified: meeting personal needs, living with the consequences of an 'othered' identity, connection and recognition, and relationships and advocacy. Autistic adults reported many barriers to feeling that they belonged in a number of social spaces and the detrimental effect this had on their well-being. Fundamental to positive narratives of well-being, were feelings of connection and recognition from others and positive accepting relationships, with autistic-led spaces, particularly the Autscape conference, being frequently cited as of central significance in increasing feelings of well-being and belonging. This study has demonstrated a need for less focus on remediation and more on limiting the social isolation of autistic people.

Introduction

Ever since Durkheim's (1897) seminal work, social scientific theorists have debated the potential link between well-being and social belonging. Attempts to improve the well-being of those diagnosed with a psychiatric condition have frequently centred upon notions of the remediation of a functionally normative social agent to enable return to previously held societal roles (Parsons, 1951). Despite variations in definition, well-being is generally assumed to encompass subjective evaluation of physical, mental, social and spiritual life experiences (Friedli, 2009). However, there are questions that warrant closer examination: what do well-being and social belonging mean for someone on the autism spectrum?1 How are they practically achieved?

Studies using well-being indicators with adults on the autism spectrum often feature limited self-assessment measures (Bracher, 2014) and the extent to which standardised measures of well-being capture autistic experience and sensibilities is debatable (Robertson, 2010):

> *'Most scales devised for use with the general population cannot be used with all population sub-sets.'*
> (International Wellbeing Group, 2013, 5)

Current measures of well-being used in the context of autism have been developed with a non-autistic population and hence cannot be assumed to adequately reflect an autistic perspective, although this area of research has recently been gaining increasing attention (Billstedt, *et al*, 2011; Burgess & Gustein, 2007, Renty & Roeyers, 2006; Robertson, 2010). Renty and Roeyers (2006) highlighted the need for people on the autism spectrum to have access to support networks, as well as effective professional back-up, following a comprehensive needs assessment. Burgess and Gustein (2007) suggested that well-being measures could be broken down into 'social functioning', such as quality of friendships and availability of social support networks, and 'emotional functioning', such as self-esteem and mental health. Billstedt *et al* (2011) found there was a need for improvements in occupational and recreational activities accessed by people on the autism spectrum and suggested that more research was needed into the concept of an 'autism-friendly environment' including the development of well-being assessment tools designed to be relevant to the particular needs of people on the autism spectrum.

Robertson (2010), an American autistic researcher, critiqued deficit model assumptions about well-being for autistic people, and suggested an alternative perspective based on the concept of neurodiversity. Rather than seeing autistic people as 'broken' and in need of 'fixing', such a perspective would focus on diversity of need, and personal 'strengths' as well as 'challenges'. Robertson (2010) suggests that Schalock's (2000) quality of life framework is a good starting point for building a model for viewing core domains of well-being for autistic adults, and highlights the need to develop a collaborative approach between professionals and autistic adults if meaningful solutions are to be found to meet the challenges that autistic people face in navigating social life. Schalock (2000) reviewed research relating to quality of life measures over a 30-year period and identified eight core domains, with relevant indicators: self-determination (autonomy, decision-making, self-direction), social inclusion (acceptance, status, community activity), material well-being (ownership, employment), personal development (education, personal competence), emotional well-being (spirituality, safety, freedom from stress), interpersonal relations (intimacy, friendship, support), rights (privacy, voting, access) and physical well-being (health, nutrition, recreation). Robertson (2010) describes Schalock's (2000) model as a non-normative approach compatible with a social model of disability, and accepting of diversity and individual efforts toward self-determination and self-advocacy. Although supporting the non-normative approach of Schalock (2000), however, Robertson's (2010) own use of terms such as 'strengths' and 'challenges' could be seen as conceptually embedded in normative thinking.

Theorists such as Timimi *et al* (2011) and Runswick-Cole (2014) have questioned the use of medicalised labels such as autism and also concepts such as neurodiversity, and the possible detrimental effects of a politics of identity. In contrast, research conducted by Beardon and Edmonds (2007) found that 83% of autistic adults they surveyed identified one of their greatest challenges as being a lack of understanding and recognition of their differing needs from other people. The same issue was highlighted by autistic children and young people in consultation exercises undertaken in the development of materials by Milton and Giannadou (2012). Milton (2012; 2014) has theorised previously that such gaps in understanding arise from differing dispositional perceptions and ways of being in life, a mismatch of what is salient or of interest within any given context, the 'double empathy problem'. For Robertson (2010), when professionals look at the barriers autistic people face in social life, they rarely focus on how social attitudes and norms can create them. One of many examples Robertson (2010) gives refers to autistic people attaining and sustaining employment, where efforts are often concerned with adapting the autistic employee to fit into social contexts rather than adapting such contexts to meet the needs of the individual.

The study

Our small-scale exploratory study sought to develop an understanding of the meaning of well-being and social belonging as represented within the narratives of adults on the autism spectrum. Employing an interpretivist approach facilitates the investigation of potential contributory factors to these lived experiences in order to inform further research regarding both this topic and service provision for adults on the autism spectrum.

The project involved a thematic analysis of issues of the magazine *Asperger United* (AU). AU was founded in 1993 and is run by and for adults on the autism spectrum, although some parents subscribe to it on behalf of their children. Since 2000, AU has been supported by the National Autistic Society. Themes and issues relevant to adults on the spectrum and expressed through the articles within AU were collated and analysed, with particular attention given to references made to factors that have influenced, either positively or negatively, an individual's sense of well-being or social belonging, as well as any links made in narratives between these two constructs. Although AU magazine is accessed by people across the autism spectrum, as the title of the magazine suggests, it is engaged with primarily by those with a good linguistic understanding. Not all contributors would identify with the term 'Asperger syndrome', however, and so the wider terms of 'autism', 'autistic' and 'autistic spectrum' have been used as descriptors in this study.

Methods

Research question

What is the meaning of well-being and belonging for autistic adults?

Sampling

At the time of analysis, 79 editions of AU had been published. Twenty-one editions of AU were sampled from the issues available from the National Autistic Society information service, ranging over a six-year period from issue 54 (April 2008) through to issue 78 (April 2014). Issues including articles written by the researchers were excluded from the study (issues 71, 72 and 79). Issues more than six years old were also excluded in order to keep the project analysis manageable and current. AU contributions are accepted in the form of articles, letters to the editor, book reviews and pen pals. All textual information within these sections was analysed for this study; in total 78 articles, 81 letters to the editor, 37 reviews, 121 penpal entries and 44 announcements were analysed.

Analysis

Thematic analysis was selected for data analysis because, located within the interpretivist paradigm, it can be used to produce in-depth interpretative analyses, providing nuanced and complex interpretations of data (Clarke & Braun, 2013). The analytic process involved progressing from a description of the data to an interpretive account of the themes that emerged from the analysis to a discussion of their wider implications. The first author undertook first-order coding of the data, viewing the data-set a number of times for familiarity before labelling basic segments of the text. The data were coded using descriptive markers, to allow as much as possible for meanings to 'emerge' from the data. Following the methodology of Braun and Clarke (2006), these first-order themes were strongly linked to the data and were inductive in nature, without a predetermined frame of reference, in an attempt to limit the effects of personal preconceptions. These first-order themes were then organised into meaningful groups under the second stage of the coding (Tuckett, 2005). Sub-themes were formed from this process through interpreting the data with reference to the notions of well-being and belonging. Finally, sub-themes were combined into meaningful clusters to develop four overarching themes. Throughout this process, the first author reflected upon possible ways that he had been affected by the process and upon his own positionality and potential bias in interpretations made. The second author then reviewed themes, subthemes and codes and further developed them to ensure internal coherence and avoid repetition between themes.

Epistemology

Influenced by the interpretive paradigm, a thematic analysis was utilised in order to capture patterns in both the lived experiences as perceived by adults on the autism spectrum and the wider discourse that they draw upon, thus acknowledging how people make meaning from their lived experiences. The interpretivist paradigm emphasises the importance of contextualised analysis: through drawing on the wider discourse, the data are interpreted and patterns identified (Gephart, 1999). However, it is recognised that interpretation of the data is infused with the concerns of the researchers.

Ethical issues

This study originated from discussions with members of the advisory committee for Research Autism and received ethical approval from the National Association of Disability Practitioners. An important ethical issue was encountered, however, in the decision to conduct a thematic analysis of AU magazine. Despite AU being publicly available, within the autistic community there has been upset and anger expressed at how scholars in the field of autism have misinterpreted autistic community and culture, through 'quote-mining' – finding quotes to fit one's own agenda (Arnold, 2012) – and 'fishbowling' – invasively inspecting and misinterpreting autistic culture from a privileged position of academic power (Moon, as quoted in Milton & Moon, 2012). In a study of this nature, it is inevitable that the interpretation will be partial and influenced by researcher positionality. If any of the submissions to AU have been misframed in this analysis, the authors apologise and hope that this does not cause upset. Readers are advised to read the writings of autistic people through public media such as AU and engage with autistic culture and the concerns of autistic people.

Results

The thematic analysis identified four main themes that encompassed a large number of sub-themes.

Theme 1. Meeting personal needs

The theme of 'meeting personal needs' was developed from writers in AU's expressions of needs relating to embodying an autistic disposition within social settings. The term 'personal needs' is used to emphasise the individuality of these needs and related experiences. Personal needs encompassed those relating to minimising stress and fulfilling one's own needs and desires.

Stress reduction

A personal need often mentioned with regard to minimising stress was that of having structure and routine in one's life. It should be said, however, that the structures which led to the most subjective benefit to well-being were structures that originated from the autistic person themselves, rather than those that were externally imposed. Another common personal need related to managing stress was the avoidance of sensory overload:

> *'It makes me a very visible case of 'sensory issues', when a*
> *spectrumite's body is discomforted by certain clothes and fabrics.'*
> (Maurice, 'Sensitivity and Clothing', issue 66, 4)

On occasion, however, these intrinsic needs were set within a social context with comments referring to society as being too fast paced or not accommodating a slow and deliberate style of processing or thinking, with some commenting on a preference for a rural lifestyle. The need for quiet time alone was often mentioned, yet this was set in juxtaposition with a need for connection (see the third theme).

Personal fulfilment

A number of contributors to AU mentioned the need to express their spirituality, yet many had met with discrimination and stigma within spiritual communities. A number of contributors specifically mentioned Buddhism or techniques such as mindfulness. Personal fulfilment was also discussed in relation to sexuality. Many contributors to AU magazine talked of being part of the lesbian, gay, bisexual and transgender community and the intersectional issues that were brought up for them.

The most predominant issue in relation to personal fulfilment was being able to engage in pursuits of interest. Of note was also how engagement with such activities of interest led many to report on feelings that could be described as a 'flow state' (characterised by being 'in the moment' and totally focused on the activity at hand) (McDonnell & Milton, 2014):

> *'I have always been happiest when absorbed in very detailed*
> *problem solving.'* (Tom, 'Work Detail', issue 66, 10)

This theme highlights the importance of structure and routine in minimising stress for people on the autism spectrum. However, it also brings attention to the importance of these structures and routines being devised by individuals and not imposed on them by external forces. Indeed, externally imposed structures may not be conducive to the lifestyles favoured by the writers in AU. Furthermore, when engaging in interests or addressing spiritual needs within these societal structures, ostracism may be experienced, perhaps explaining why people on the autism may describe desires to connect with others yet can highly value time spent alone.

Theme 2. Living with the consequences of an 'othered' identity

The theme of 'living with the consequences of an 'othered' identity' referred to a large number of issues, categorised as societal othering, self-discovery and social navigation.

Societal othering

Societal othering encompassed issues including being excluded from social activities, attempts of others to 'normalise behaviour', problems with authority figures (expectations of obedience and conformity), stigma and bullying.

Bullying was almost universally reported on as an experience in school life, but it was also reported on as happening within the family, in further and higher education, and often within workplace environments. Living with such an 'othered' identity was also linked to feelings of isolation and social alienation, and mental ill-health such as social anxiety and depression. Many reported a sense of what could be described as 'psycho-emotional disablement' (Milton and Lyte 2012; Reeve 2011) between their own sense of self and the presentation of self expected from others:

> 'Growing up in this way, it can lead to feeling as though we are 'wrong' or 'defective', and for me that led to low self-esteem and depression, as well as an intense need to find a way to improve myself and make myself acceptable to others.' (Sian, 'Asperger's and Anorexia', issue 68, 15)

> 'Throughout my life I have developed an 'act' to be 'normal', which has allowed me to interact with people, but this negates the possibility of friendship due to the fact it's not the real me.' (Robert, 'Relationships', issue 77, 16)

Unfortunately, despite a small number of contributors to AU talking of positive encounters and relationships with psych-professionals, interactions of this nature were often seen as extremely negative, with many reporting that their needs were not recognised or were misinterpreted, with some saying that they were forced by such professionals into actions they did not want. Others reported how they were blocked from seeing their families or made more ill by being under psychiatric surveillance, with one contributor to AU stating how one psychiatrist had labelled them as 'evil'.

> *'I formed a high regard for all the therapists; however, none had experience of treating a person with AS so that, in some respects, their efforts were ineffective or even counter-productive.'* (Tony, 'Anxious Thoughts', issue 76, 4)

Another source of difficulty associated with living with an othered identity was problems in gaining and sustaining employment. This was related to various issues, including one's thoughts being at odds with other people, not being able to achieve the qualifications that their ability warranted, being undervalued at work, a lack of job satisfaction, social alienation at work and underemployment through skills not being recognised:

> *'I had the same to offer employers as other students looking for work, I was only ever offered the worst paid and hardest temporary positions in factories such as working in a noisy dairy or packing department whilst a friend landed office work.'* (Richard, 'The Challenges of Employment', issue 74, 12)

> *'I work in retail, which is a notoriously pressured environment. It seems to proliferate with NTs who have no insight into their behaviour, let alone understand anyone else's.'* (Anon, letter to the editor, issue 75, 14)

Although some contributors to AU mentioned difficulties in terms of understanding the intentions of others within social interactions, it was far more common that a lack of understanding from others was of more difficulty, indicative of what Milton (2012; 2014) and Chown (2014) have previously theorised as the double empathy problem:

> *'Yet NTs find it impossible to empathise with us.'* (Robert, letter to the editor, issue 74, 9)

In the following passage there is also the problem of the 'dyspathic' (Cameron 2012) reactions from others expressed:

> *'Equally, if empathy is all about social alignment, it is not just about creating 'Me and Us', but also about creating 'Us and Them'. It is normal for empathy to be selective, local, partial: typically people distribute their empathy in socially determined patterns.'* (Dinah Murray, 'Empathy – Handle with Care!', issue 76, 14)

Such interactions can lead to a downturn in trust and rapport with others and subsequent effects on feelings of well-being and belonging:

'When I am in an environment I feel comfortable in, with people who are kind and tolerant, and doing things I enjoy, then I am as happy as the next person. It is when people tell me I should think, speak or behave differently that I start to feel different, upset, isolated and worthless. So surely the problem is a lack of fit with the environment rather than something inside my brain that needs to be fixed?' (Victoria, 'Are You Taking Something for It?', issue 76, 12)

Self-discovery

A generally more positive aspect of living with an 'othered' identity for many contributors to AU was the influence of gaining a diagnosis. Many felt that this led to a greater sense of self-understanding and understanding of others. Issues remained for many, however; for instance, the perceived under-diagnosis of women, or a felt disjuncture between how an individual saw themselves and how others treated them:

'The years of depression, cutting, starving and being sick were a reaction to a confused and anxious mind, trying to cope with being [an undiagnosed] Aspie in an NT world.' (Sian, 'Asperger's and Anorexia', issue 68, 15)

In terms of personal identity a diversity of views were expressed, from those wishing to not be defined by their 'disability' and who preferred to talk of 'people with autism' to those who saw autism as an inseparable part of their identity to be accepted and/or celebrated. Many also talked of having been on a personal journey, moving from hating 'their autism', to seeing themselves as a 'person with autism' to an 'autistic person', via their further engagement with autistic culture and community:

'When I first learned about autism, I wanted nothing to do with it. Then, that led to me reluctantly accepting it just wasn't going anywhere, and I called myself a person with autism. Now, though, I think of myself as an autistic person, with a family of other autistic people (even if we are far apart).' (Amanda, 'Autscape', issue 76, 14)

Most importantly, however, nearly all wanted to be able to define themselves on their own terms, and be better understood as an individual.

Social navigation

This refers to the social practices needed to navigate a social environment when one has an 'othered', or as Goffman (1963) would state, 'spoiled identity' and to the management strategies available to people occupying such a social position. Many talked of finding safe and accepting social spaces within their lives in order to retreat from the social spaces where they felt ostracised:

> *'Far from being loners, most of us are lonely.'* (Ruth, 'Relationships', issue 77, 14)

> *'I started attending a social group for people with autism. It has helped a great deal with my confidence.'* (Paul, 'Family on the Spectrum', issue 67, 20)

Others talked of how they needed to prepare themselves for tackling an unforgiving environment. A large number of contributors to AU commented upon the issue of 'masking' or 'passing as normal'. Some talked of a learnt performance of normalcy that they wished to break away from:

> *'I was wondering how other people in the same position have 'embraced' their Asperger's personality and shed the masks that have to be worn every day – I feel that mine will have to be surgically removed, as they've grown to be a big but uncomfortable and ill-fitting part of me.'* (Karen, letter to the editor, issue 76, 20)

Others described how creating a facade of normality that subsumed their sense of authentic self resulted in psychological damage:

> *'Help should be sought if mental-health problems are suspected, but I was diagnosed with depression when what was wrong with me was misguided attempts to conform to the norm.'* (Rob, letter to the editor, issue 75, 18; original emphasis)

> *'Some contributors to AU rejected the need to pass as normal and instead promoted a sense of 'autistic pride': We want to show people that autistic adults are autonomous; we want to speak for ourselves and we want to change the presumption that we need others to speak for us.'* (Kabie, 'The ARGH Autism Alert Card', issue 68, 11)

Some talked of the minor advantages to passing within specific, but temporary, social interactions:

> *'The autistic spectrum is so wide that I know many of you will be reading this thinking, 'Oh, I don't need social skills training', but some people do, especially around bullying.'* (Robyn Steward, 'Too Sane for this World?', issue 76, 9)

This theme presents a complex and transactional challenge to developing positive and meaningful relationships between autistic and non-autistic individuals. Running through this is a thread that non-autistic people have difficulties understanding the viewpoints of autistic people, resulting in mistreatment such as bullying, social alienation and marginalisation in healthcare and employment settings. It is perhaps unsurprising then that autistic individuals feel that developing trust and rapport is difficult to achieve, compounding these difficulties. However, the experience of receiving a diagnosis could be seen to counteract some of these negative experiences, resulting in more empathic understanding from others.

The need to pathologise autism in order to receive acceptance by non-autistic people may, however, provide further evidence for the 'othering' and alienation experienced by people on the autism spectrum. The practice of 'masking' or 'passing as normal' could be viewed as a highly adaptive response to this: faced with either being ostracised for 'being different' or being 'accepted' by pathologising one's identity through a medical diagnosis, 'acting' in a way to avoid either of these outcomes seems a logical strategy.

Theme 3. Connection and recognition

The third theme 'connection and recognition' pertains to when adults on the autistic spectrum had found a sense of connection and recognition with/from others, a sense of well-being and belonging, and better understanding of their subjective viewpoint from those around them.

Sharing

Often commented upon was the need and/or satisfaction gained from the ability to share one's interests, often with 'like-minded' others. Indeed, this was the primary theme of the pen-pal section of AU magazine and a number of articles:

> 'I would like to speak to people my own age or a little bit older. I like to talk to people with similar interests.' (Lyssa, Pen Pal 113, issue 69, 9)

> 'I cannot talk about my real experience of life to most people, because they wouldn't understand or be interested. That makes me feel, as the saying goes, 'lonely in a room full of people' and I'm fed up with it. I would like to talk to caring, intelligent, honest people who understand Asperger's well and with whom I can talk openly. My hobbies include cycling, walking in the countryside, and rational thinking.' (Daniel, Pen Pal 95, issue 68, 7)

Highly valued by many was the opportunity to share with others identifying themselves as being on the autism spectrum. This included the use of online forums, the space provided by AU magazine itself and particularly the opportunity to meet in-person with others on the autism spectrum. This included local social groups and conferences led by autistic people, in particular the annual Autscape conference.

Acceptance

When 'autistic spaces' such as the Autscape conference were commented upon, the narrative soon altered significantly: notions of mutual acceptance and empathy with others, feeling less isolated, building friendships, meeting new people, having control over the 'discourse', enjoyment of leisure activities, acceptance of difference, interaction aides, commonality and 'love' were all mentioned:

> *'As in previous Autscapes, I found the spontaneous discussions to be even more interesting that the scheduled presentations, as the spontaneous discussions allowed me to get to know other autistics, to explore our commonalities and differences, and to somewhat quench my insatiable thirst for meeting other autistics and for building bridges.'* (Chen, 'Autscape 2011', issue 69, 17)

> *'When I meet my people, I know, because I feel it. And my people were there at Autscape and the whole thing was imbued with love, expressed autistically, but love nonetheless … Autscape has meant I see my differences as part of the differences that make up the whole of humanity and as something to be celebrated, not something I need to get away from … there was no fear or ridicule. I had never before experienced such a feeling of coming home.'* (Amanda, 'Autscape', issue 76, 14)

Connections with others, having one's needs recognised and feeling mutual acceptance was not limited, however, to autistic-led spaces alone. Individual contributors to AU magazine talked of other social spaces within their lives where such understanding was being achieved. However, what these quotes highlight is the felt need for people on the autism spectrum to feel safe from fear and ridicule, to be valued for their contributions, creativity and effort, and to be acknowledged. This need can be seen as analogous with the notion of 'unconditional positive regard'. For some this meant the rejection of well-being and notions of belonging as defined by an 'ableist' or 'neurotypical' society.

This theme recognises the importance of feeling a connection to other 'like-minded' people for the well-being of people on the autism spectrum. Having this connection leads to feelings of acceptance and being understood which, as described in the second theme, are feelings that many autistic people have not experienced when interacting with non-autistic people. These positive experiences of connectedness can result in feeling safe, being valued and being acknowledged, viewed by the contributors to AU as vital aspects of their well-being.

Theme 4. Relationships and advocacy

The final theme identified, 'relationships and advocacy', was concerned with friendships, intimate relationships and family. These were frequent areas of difficulty for the contributors to AU magazine, with a number of articles dedicated to this topic:

> 'Now, close personal relationships and I have what you might call a nodding acquaintance. I usually manage one every ten years or so, on average.' (Mark, 'Don't Really Go in for Titles, Best Just Read On', issue 76, 11)

External support

Relationships with mentors and tutors were valued highly when working positively for an individual. Many commented on the need for advocacy support, or in achieving their goals in life. Positive experiences in relationships such as these were remarked upon as significantly helping with issues such as mental health.

Family and personal relationships

A commonly cited sub-theme was that of family life. Accounts of relationships of family life varied greatly, but could be seen as having a marked effect on a participant's sense of well-being and belonging:

> 'We're all positive and that positivity has helped us cope with everything in life. We're a strong unit: we help others and each other.' (Paul, 'Family on the Spectrum', issue 67, 20)

Self-advocacy

There were increasing accounts through AU magazine in recent years referring to self-advocacy, autistic rights and the neurodiversity movement. Interestingly, earlier editions tended to have invites to participate in research being conducted on autistic people, whilst a later edition, however, contained an advert for contributions to the *Autonomy* journal, an academic journal led by an autistic editor. This can be seen as marking a changing engagement with knowledge production within the field of autism studies.

A Mismatch of Salience: Explorations of the nature of autism from theory to practice
© Pavilion Publishing and Media Ltd and its licensors 2017.

This theme represents the profound effects personal relationships can have on the well-being of people on the autism spectrum, both positive and negative. The growth of self-advocacy may suggest a positive shift is occurring in these relationships from the historical position of people with autism being 'done to' to more partnership working.

Reflexive analysis of the researchers' positionality

The first author is diagnosed as being on the autism spectrum, a father to an autistic son, and an academic and consultant within the field of autism. He is therefore deeply embedded in autistic culture and community. Some commentators may hold the view that being so close to the subject matter could have influenced the objectivity of the analysis. However, it could be argued that this positionality actually enabled a level of 'interactional expertise' with the experiences being expressed (Milton, 2014). In interpreting the texts, interactional expertise has provided a depth of understanding that might otherwise be unavailable and allowed an awareness of nuance that informed the interpretation of the texts. Despite the advantages of the first author's positionality in terms of the analysis conducted, a decision was taken to involve the second author in checking the interpretation and themes developed to introduce another perspective and reduce potential bias in interpretation. The second author is a children's occupational therapist who has experience working with children on the autism spectrum and their families. Previous attempts to understand well-being and experiences of belonging have therefore been as a clinician and, largely, from the perspectives of parents.

Despite excluding editions of AU magazine that included articles written by the first author, comments and references to them were found. It was humbling and motivating to observe one's own contribution to this growing culture. However, many of the challenges and barriers discussed were encountered with disheartening familiarity. It was also inspiring to read people's experiences and potentially help these stories to reach a wider audience.

Discussion

The themes identified in this study highlight the many barriers and challenges faced by people on the autism spectrum in achieving well-being and a sense of belonging. Many differing narratives have been analysed, but commonalities persist: the challenges to meeting personal needs, the impact of living with an 'othered' identity, the importance of connections with, and acceptance from, others, and issues related to relationships and advocacy. These issues were found to impact on social isolation, mental ill-health and empowerment, constructs highly relevant to well-being and belonging, in the accounts analysed.

The findings from this study support those seen in previous research. The need for support networks and effective professional support were highlighted (Renty & Roeyers, 2006), as were the quality of relationships, or lack of such quality, along with issues affecting self-esteem and mental-health (Burgess & Gustein, 2007). These accounts, however, could be seen as partial, given the wide breadth of issues highlighted in this study. It is certainly the case that more research is needed with regard to an autistic 'friendly' environment (Billstedt *et al*, 2011), yet perhaps a good starting point for such research would be autistic-led social spaces such as Autscape. The findings from this study also indicate that thinking of autistic well-being purely in terms of efforts to remediate the challenges faced by autistic people as if they are a set of 'deficits' is highly limited and potentially counterproductive (as many accounts spoke of needs unrecognised or misinterpreted by professionals). This would support wider criticisms of a medical model of autism, yet questions whether the terms 'autism' and 'neurodiversity' always lead to negative consequences for people so identifying. Whilst internalising a medical model view of autism as part of one's self-identity can be potentially harmful, as argued by Timimi *et al* (2011) and Runswick-Cole (2014), reclaiming the label and associated concepts as well as connections made with people with similar dispositions can be beneficial.

The results from this study have highlighted similar issues to that of Robertson (2010), and would similarly suggest that the concept of 'neurodiversity' can help autistic and non-autistic people alike to focus on the diversity of needs people have, their strengths and interests as well as challenges. Many of the core domains suggested by Schalock (2000) were also highlighted in this study, and as Robertson (2010) suggests would make a good starting framework for analysing quality of life and well-being for autistic people. Such domains are no different from the core domains of well-being for non-autistic people, so is there a need to develop new quality of life assessment tools relevant to the particular needs of autistic people (Billstedt *et al*, 2011)? Perhaps not; however, assumptions of what may help improve quality of life and well-being for autistic people based on remedial efforts to try and improve 'functioning' by non-autistic standards are likely to be misplaced. Perhaps standardised measures could be used without much adaptation, yet what interventions researchers explore in order to improve feelings of well-being in the perceptions of autistic people may need to focus on the personal constructions and interests of the autistic person, rather than being based on normative assumptions.

Autistic identities can be said to be constructed within a context of an uneven distribution of power, with a medicalised view of autistic difference and remediation often acting as a hindrance to feelings of well-being and belonging. Issues such as 'masking' and 'passing' become a conflicted discursive space, in which some feel that it is at times easier to conform (although with great difficulty), whereas others feel unable to do so or perceive attempts to do so as inherently disabling.

The findings from this study raise questions regarding the validity of the mentalising theory of autism (Baron-Cohen, 1995; Frith, 1989), and social skills training that does not take account of autistic dispositions and subjectivity. As with previous studies (Beardon & Edmonds, 2007; Milton & Giannadou, 2012), the lack of understanding from non-autistic people in recognising the needs of autistic people as perceived by autistic people can have a seriously deleterious effect on well-being and self-esteem. Reducing the 'double empathy problem' (Chown, 2014; Milton, 2012; 2014) may mean raising autism 'awareness' based on the lived experiences of autistic people and the concept of 'neurodiversity' (Robertson, 2010), rather than purely medical model remedial explanations. People who are navigating their lives within such social/situational and discursive conditions have much to manage. The opportunities created by AU magazine, Autscape and other such autistic-led spaces are obviously beneficial to many, yet so are relationships that accept and celebrate one's way of being in the world, wherever such relationships are fostered and nurtured.

One possible problem in this study was, as mentioned previously, the influence of the social positionality and view of the researcher on the interpretation of the data. Some issues of well-being and belonging may have been considered too 'obvious' to a cultural insider. It is also important to note that contributions to AU magazine are selected by the editor, who also proposes potential themes for future issues, and therefore some of the data analysed in this project reflect an element of editorial selection.

Conclusion

This study sought to explore the meanings of well-being and social belonging for adults on the autism spectrum in an attempt to develop understanding about how to realistically achieve these. Employing an interpretivist approach, using thematic analysis to understand the accounts presented within AU, resulted in the identification of themes related to: meeting personal needs within social settings; the impact of societal othering; finding connection and recognition; and managing relationships with friends and family. Whilst these themes highlighted many of the challenges faced by people on the autism spectrum in achieving well-being and belonging, they also indicated that thinking of autistic well-being purely in terms of efforts to remediate challenges is counterproductive. Moreover, reclaiming the label and associated concepts and making connections with people with similar dispositions can be beneficial.

The findings from this research may not be representative of the views and experiences of a wider constituency of adults on the autism spectrum, but do indicate potential issues and priorities of those within the autistic community who are verbally articulate, and as a group are likely to have experienced forms of social exclusion, or at least misinterpretation of their social experiences and felt needs (Milton, 2012; 2014). The results of this study are useful for those considering what to measure, and how, in terms of well-being for future studies. This in turn could help inform practical approaches for supporting people on the autism spectrum in adult life. It must be remembered, however, that this study is but a snapshot of expressions from a number of adults on the autism spectrum, and can only highlight a number of main themes and issues, which can somewhat disguise some of the nuances contained within individual personal stories.

This study has brought attention to the many commonalities in what contributes towards well-being for both autistic and non-autistic people. However, it has also highlighted the considerable differences in the barriers to achieving it. This study has demonstrated a need for less focus on remediation and more focus on limiting the social isolation of autistic people.

Note

In accordance with other 'autistic voices' (Sainsbury, 2000; Sinclair, 1993), this article will use the descriptors 'autistic person/people' and 'autistic spectrum'.

Disclosure statement

No potential conflict of interest was reported by the authors.

References

Arnold L (2012) Autism (book review). *Disability and Society* **27** (5) 729–730.

Baron-Cohen S (1995) *Mindblindness: An essay on autism and theory of mind*. Bradford: MIT Press.

Beardon L & Edmonds G (2007) *The ASPECT Consultancy Report: A national report on the needs of adults with Asperger syndrome*. Sheffield: Sheffield Hallam University.

Billstedt E, Gillberg I & Gillberg C (2011) Aspects of Quality of Life in Adults Diagnosed with Autism in Childhood: A population-based study. *Autism* **15** (1) 7–20.

Bracher M (2014) *ADRC Service Evaluation and Development Project: Post-diagnostic service development study*. Isle of Wight: ADRC.

Braun V & Clarke V (2006) Using Thematic Analysis in Psychology. *Qualitative Research in Psychology* **3** 77–101.

Burgess A & Gustein S (2007) Quality of Life for People with Autism: Raising the standard for evaluating successful outcomes. *Child and Adolescent Mental Health* **12** 80–86.

Cameron L (2012) *Dyspathy: The dynamic complement of empathy*. Milton Keynes: The Open University.

Chown N (2014) More on the Ontological Status of Autism and Double Empathy. *Disability and Society* **29** (10) 1672–1676.

Clarke V & Braun V (2013) Teaching thematic analysis: overcoming challenges and developing strategies for effective learning. *The Psychologist* **26** (2) 120–123.

Durkheim E (1897/1972) *Suicide*. London: Sage.

Friedli L (2009) *Mental Health, Resilience and Inequalities*. Denmark: World Health Organisation – Europe Branch.

Frith U (1989) *Autism: Explaining the enigma*. London: Wiley-Blackwell.

Gephart R (1999) Paradigms and Research Methods. Research Methods Forum: 4. International Wellbeing Group. 2006. *Personal Wellbeing Index*. Melbourne: Australian Centre on Quality of Life, Deakin University.

Goffman E (1963) *Stigma: Notes on the management of a spoiled identity*. Simon & Schuster.

International Wellbeing Group (2013). *Personal Wellbeing Index* – Adult [online]. Available at: www.acqol.com.au/iwbg/wellbeing-index/pwi-a-english.pdf (accessed October 2017).

McDonnell A & Milton D (2014) Going with the Flow: Reconsidering 'repetitive behaviour' through the concept of 'flow states'.' In: G Jones and E Hurley (Eds) *Good Autism Practice: Autism, happiness and wellbeing*, 58–63. Edgbaston: British Institute of Learning Disabilities.

Milton D (2012) On the ontological status of autism: the 'double empathy problem'. *Disability and Society* **27** (6) 883–887.

Milton D (2014) Autistic expertise: a critical reflection on the production of knowledge in autism studies'. *Autism: The International Journal of Research and Practice* **18** (7) 794–802.

Milton D & Giannadou K (2012) *Views of Children and Young People with Autism On: What makes a good school for pupils with autism* [online]. London: Autism Education Trust. Available at: www.aettraininghubs.org.uk/wp-content/uploads/2012/05/2.3-33.2-Pupils-views-on-school.pdf (accessed September 2017).

Milton D & Moon L (2012) The normalisation agenda and the psycho-emotional disablement of autistic people. *Autonomy: The Journal of Critical Interdisciplinary Autism Studies* **1** (1).

Milton D & Moon L (2012) And that Damian is what I call life changing: findings from an action research project involving autistic adults in an online sociology group. *Good Autism Practice* **7** (2) 78–86.

Parsons T (1951) *The Social System*. New York: The Free Press.

Reeve D (2011) Ableism within Disability Studies: The myth of the reliable and contained body'. *Theorising Normalcy and the Mundane, 2nd International Conference 15/09/11*. Manchester: Manchester Metropolitan University.

Renty J & Roeyers H (2006) Quality of life in high-functioning adults with autistic spectrum disorder: the predictive value of disability and support characteristics. *Autism* **10** (5) 511–524.

Robertson S (2010) Neurodiversity, quality of life and autistic adults: shifting research and professional focuses onto real-life challenges. *Disability Studies Quarterly* **30** (1).

Runswick-Cole K (2014) 'Us' and 'them': the limits and possibilities of a 'politics of neurodiversity' in neoliberal times. *Disability and Society* **29** (7) 1117–1129.

Sainsbury, C. (2000) *Martian in the Playground: Understanding the Schoolchild with Asperger's Syndrome*. Bristol: Lucky Duck.

Schalock R (2000) Three decades of quality of life. *Focus on Autism and Other Developmental Disabilities* **15** 116–127.

Sinclair J (1993) *Don't Mourn for Us* [online]. Available at: http://www.autreat.com/dont_mourn.html (accessed September 2017).

Timimi S, Gardner N & McCabe B (2011) *The Myth of Autism*. Basingstoke: Palsgrave.

Tuckett A (2005) The care encounter: pondering caring, honest communication and control. *International Journal of Nursing Practice* **11** (2) 77–84.

Educational discourse and the autistic student: a study using Q-sort methodology

(thesis summary)

Abstract

With some notable exceptions (e.g. Jones *et al*, 2012), current guidance regarding best practice for the education of children on the autism spectrum often reflects a medical / behavioural model approach that seeks to remediate perceived deficits (Cumine *et al*, 1998; Hanbury, 2005; Hewitt, 2005; Worth, 2005; Hagland & Webb, 2009). Such advice can be contrasted with that given by autistic writers (Sainsbury, 2000; Lawson, 2010) often situating itself within a social model of disability. This study utilised Q-sort methodology (n = 60), followed by qualitative interviews (n = 6) to investigate the ideology and priorities of differing stakeholders, including autistic adults, parents of autistic children, practitioners and academics working in the field, and those occupying multiple positions, regarding the education of autistic pupils of secondary-school age. Eight factors were extracted through the PoetQ application for analysis. Two of these factors were dominant within the data-set. One represented a critical radical pedagogy frequently favoured by autistic adults, the other an approach akin to a Positive Behavioural Support (PBS) model often preferred by non-autistic parents. Practitioners and academics were found to hold a less-defined eclectic approach between these two main factors. The article concludes with a reflection regarding this 'three-way dispositional problem' and offers a number of recommendations for future research and practice.

Introduction

Ever since autism first appeared as a clinical descriptor in the work of Leo Kanner and Hans Asperger in the 1940s, parental activism has often focussed on the educational needs of their autistic children (Waltz, 2013). Such a focus has led to many educational models of intervention, with a variety of views regarding the educational challenges faced by autistic people being expressed (Sainsbury, 2000; Jones, 2002; Jones *et al*, 2008). A great deal of the advice offered by educational literature regarding autistic pupils and students employs a medical, behavioural, or cognitive psychological, model to inform their practices (Cumine *et al*, 1998; Hanbury, 2005; Hewitt, 2005; Worth, 2005; Hagland & Webb, 2009). Such examples describe educational practices as 'interventions' and as 'remedial' and 'compensatory', focusing only on perceived functional deficits, whilst not acknowledging the possibility of autistic strengths or making an attempt to harness them; the lack of such a focus, is of concern to autistic writers such as Sainsbury (2000), as well as academics such as Jordan (2009).

Despite many years of research into the educational needs of autistic children however, little evidence has been gathered on the views of autistic children and young people themselves regarding their educational priorities and even less on the views of autistic adults who may have useful experiential knowledge to impart. When views have been published, they often present a largely social model of disability (Senior & Viveash, 1998), as is the case by Sainsbury (2000), although a diversity of views can be found across all stakeholder groups (Humphrey & Lewis, 2008). Sainsbury (2000) argued that teachers need a greater awareness of autistic learning styles and that Further Education, Higher Education, and work opportunities needed further investigation. In a systematic review conducted for the National Council for Special Education (NCSE), Parsons *et al*, (2009), found that within the surveyed empirical research between 2002 and 2008, articles focusing on early-intervention strategies and behavioural approaches for autistic children, were dominant. Parsons *et al*. (2009) found a serious lack of research concerning the educational needs of older children and adults, or research concerning the 'autistic voice' regarding educational practices. This conclusion is also supported by a review completed on behalf of the Autism Education Trust (Jones *et al* 2008).

When one looks at parental accounts of living with an autistic child, accounts vary from those framed within a highly medical / behavioural model (Maurice, 1993) to those far more akin to a social model approach (Zurcher, 2012; Lilley, 2015). Whilst parent narratives regarding the education of their children are somewhat valorised in educational discourse (e.g. through their narratives being included in setting goals for Individual Education Plans (IEP)), many parents still feel that their views are not taken account of fully (ABA4all, 2014; Lilley, 2015).

Research Questions:
- ■ What discourses are being used by relevant stakeholders in the narrative construction of views about educational priorities for autistic children of secondary school age?

■ What commonalities and tensions exist between (and within) the subjective constructions of stakeholders regarding the education of autistic children of secondary school age?

Methodology

This study utilised Q-sort methodology devised by Stephenson (1935; 1953), as a way of analysing personal experience and subjectivity. The methodology involves participants sorting and ordering a set number of items (usually statements about a topic). Through the sorting process, participants provide a visual representation of their viewpoint, which can then be compared and contrasted with those of other participants in order to pull out common factors (ideal models of common threads running through differing perspectives). This process is followed up by discussions, which can be analysed qualitatively and compared with findings from a statistical analysis of the ranking exercise.

The first aspect of designing a Q-sort methodological study is the definition of the topic concourse. Not to be confused with a discourse, the concourse refers to the collection of all possible discourses pertaining to a topic. Thus a concourse includes all the relevant aspects of all the discourses available on a topic. An indication of the concourse was obtained from literature regarding educational ideology and practice, both in general (e.g. Scrimshaw, 1983) and from literature specifically regarding the education of pupils on the autism spectrum (Jones *et al*, 2012). For the purposes of this study, forty-two statements (the Q-set) of opinion were generated reflecting the spread of views across the concourse. The statements were selected to try and represent the range of views encountered in the literature.

Whenever a Q-set is designed, different structures and samples would be selected by different researchers from the available concourse, yet this is not regarded as a problem for Q-sort methodology. Firstly, whatever the starting point of statements is, the aim is to provide a range of statements as indicative as one can of the range of opinions available about a topic. Secondly, irrespective of which statements are chosen for the Q-set, it is the research participants who ultimately give meaning to the statements in the sorting process and following discussion (Brown, 1980; Thomas & Baas, 1992; Watts & Stenner, 2012).

'The perfect Q set is probably a thing of fantasy and fiction.' (Watts & Stenner, 2012:63)

Whilst the selection of Q-set statements cannot be said to be a truly representative sample of views, the Q-sort method allows participants to rank statements in the order of their choosing and to interpret the statements in idiosyncratic ways, the in-depth meanings of which need to be analysed through the statistical and qualitative data generated from the Q-sort method.

The final set of statements was broken down into 10 categories of 4 statements each, followed by a final two general statements. The structure of this categorisation is shown below:

General category	General topic	Number of statements
Ideological	Classical Humanist	4
	Liberal Humanist	4
	Progressive	4
	Radical Pedagogy	4
Practice-based	Behaviourist	4
	Functionalist	4
	Relationship Development Intervention (RDI)	4
	Interactionist	4
Practical areas	Building relationships	4
	Enabling environments	4
General statements	The need for a tailored curriculum	1
	The need for evidence-based practice	1
Total number of statements		42

The follow-up interview questions utilised a semi-structured and open-ended format, allowing for flexibility of response and rich and detailed qualitative data to be produced, regarding constructions of educational experiences.

Sampling for this study consisted of opportunity sampling for each participant sub-category: autistic adults, parents of secondary-aged children on the autism spectrum, and practitioners and academics working in the field of autism and education. For each of these groupings it was hoped that at least between 5 and 10 participants could be found, in order to give as wider breadth of opinion as possible inputting into the extraction of the Q-sort factor analysis. Participants were recruited via the University of Birmingham students studying autism within the School of Education, through autistic-led organisations and online forums, and from local and national parent-focused organisations. A standardised recruitment letter was designed and sent out to these various sites. Participants were given clear guidance as to the nature and aims of the study and statements regarding consent to complete. Sixty participants (including the researcher) agreed to take part in the study:

Range of participants	Number of participants within sample
Autistic women	20
Autistic men	6
Non-autistic mothers of autistic children	12
Non-autistic fathers of autistic children	3
Female practitioners	19
Male practitioners	5
Autistic practitioners	7
Academics	10
Autistic academics	4
Total number of participants	60*

*Note that a number of participants held multiple positions in relation to autism

By utilising a Q-sort methodology, this study did not seek to be widely representative of the predominance of discourses/beliefs held amongst stakeholder groups, but to highlight the number of available discursive repertoires being utilised within the field, and the motives behind these being employed by various stakeholders that participate. Thus the number of participants required for the study, was that needed to adequately distinguish the number of factors/discursive repertoires in operation, and with enough rich qualitative data to critically examine these formulations and how they are used by participants from differing subject positions within the field.

For Q-sort methodological studies only a limited number of respondents are needed in order to establish the existence of a factor for comparison with one another. Yet, according to Van Exel and de Graaf (2005), a P-set (sample of participants) should provide enough breadth to maximise confidence that whatever factors are at issue will emerge from the data. For Van Exel and de Graaf (2005) the aim would be to find four or five people asserting or 'exemplifying' each anticipated viewpoint (with often 2-4, but rarely more than 6 factors tending to emerge from such data). The number of respondents aligning themselves with a factor is of much less importance to a Q-sort study, than their stakeholder position and viewpoint expressed. In a wider population, the prevalence of those associating with particular viewpoints is not measurable using this technique (Brown, 1978), but through using such techniques, the dominant viewpoints being utilised by various stakeholders can be made more explicit and examined in-depth.

The data from the ranking exercise was inputted into PQMethod software in order to compute and obtain a correlation matrix of Q-sorts. The correlation matrix measures the levels of agreement and disagreement between all individual Q-sorts in a sample compared to all other individual Q-sorts, and the distributions of rankings that each contains. This highlights the degree of similarity in points of view between participants. The correlation matrix is then open to a factor analysis that identifies the number of natural groupings of Q-sorts on the basis of similarity/dissimilarity. This gives an indication of how many factors (or discourses) are in operation within the Q-set (indicative of the concourse). Then a factor loading is determined for each Q-sort to highlight the extent to which each Q-sort is associated with each factor. The next step in the analysis involved a process of factor rotation. In this study, a *'VARIMAX'* rotation was used due to the high numbers of participants that took part in the study. Rotation of factors does not affect the original Q-sorts or relationships between Q-sorts, but changes the vantage point from which they are viewed. All of the above procedures were undertaken by utilising PQMethod software and data outputs and thus free from researcher bias, other than potential bias in the selection of the Q-set of statements from the available concourse of views available.

Due to the methodological insights of Stephenson (1953), each Q-sort does not change in position, only the point at which one views the data from. This can be done by comparing one factor with another (up to as many factors that are found within the data). Each resulting final factor represents a grouping of views (Q-sorts) that are highly correlated with one another and uncorrelated with others to a statistically significant degree. The data produced by PQMethod software also gives the estimated influence each factor had on the data set as a whole, and the number of individual Q-sorts that exemplify each factor. This data then can be analysed in terms of the differences of view held by differing participants, along with demographic data taken, to indicate the influence of subject position on the discourses being voiced.

The next step in the analytical process was to analyse the factor and difference scores associated with each statement in relation to respective factors. A statements factor score refers to the normalised weighted average statement score (z-score) of respondents who define that factor. Using these Z-scores, statements are then attributed to a quasi-normal distribution, in a composite (idealised) Q sort for each factor. The resulting Q-sort represents how a hypothetical respondent with a 100% loading on that factor would have ordered all the remaining statements in the Q-sample. When these factors are found, one can then compare the original Q-sorts to see how loaded they are to different factors. When a respondents factor loading exceeds $p<0.01$ it is called a defining variable. The difference score refers to the magnitude of difference between a statements score on any two factors needed for it to be of statistical significance. When a statement's difference score exceeds this limit then it is called a distinguishing statement. A statement that statistically does not distinguish between any of the factors is called a consensus statement. Such identified factors and statements point to those that need specific attention in analysis, as through such an analysis of distinguishing and consensus statements, the study could highlight the array of differences and commonalities in discourse within and between stakeholder groups in the field of education for autistic pupils (if not the proportion of people who hold such views), and thus answer the research questions of this study. Statements that are ranked at either end of composite Q-sorts representing a factor, are called characterising statements, while distinguishing and consensus statements show differences and similarities between factors (and thus discourses).

Finally, an analysis was made of the qualitative explanations given by the participants in relation to interpreting the factors found through those provided through the PoetQ software, and triangulated with data from the analysis of the follow-up questions that participants could chose to partake in.

The participants were asked to log-on to the PoetQ software platform and read through the instructions regarding the study and conditions of consent. The right to withdraw, handling of data, right to anonymity, and the nature of the study were fully outlined, and consent attained by an online question before participants could continue with the study. Participants were then asked to sort 42 randomly numbered statements into a standardised Q-sort grid (although via an accessible process utilising PoetQ software) as shown in the following table:

Most disagree										Most agree
2										2
	4							4		
		5				5				
			6		6					
				8						

*The number in the columns depicting the number of statements allowed by a participant in their selection of statements.

The ranked statements were all in reference to: personal views regarding educational priorities for secondary school-age pupils on the autism spectrum. They were then asked to sort statements into three piles: agree, disagree, and neutral or undecided. Participants were then asked to rank the statements, utilising the PoetQ software, with all statements being ranked within this framework. The participants could then move any of the statements they so chose around the pyramid structure to their liking. Finally, participants were asked a small number of questions and whether they would like to be contacted for further input into the study. This further input took the form of the following set of semi-structured online interview questions:

1. How would you describe autism in general, for example, as a disability or difference?

2. What do you consider to be the most essential educational priorities for children on the autism spectrum, and why?

3. What would you say has influenced your view concerning educational priorities for children on the autism spectrum, and why?

4. How do you think your educational priorities can be implemented in practice?

5. Is there anything else that you would like to add?

Findings

From the Q-sort factor extraction method, eight factors were identified that statistically explained 72% of the variance in the data sets. Of these factors, two were dominant, making up 32% of the variance, with one third of the individual Q-sorts exemplifying one of these two factors (factors 1 and 2). Factors 3 to 8 contained 11 exemplifying Q-sorts between them, showing marked differences to factors 1 and 2, and 29 Q-sorts did not exemplify any of these factors, but were influenced to different degrees by each of them.

A number of participants exemplifying a factor 1 viewpoint expressed the need for a tailored curriculum. However, the language used by these participants was more akin to functionalist or behaviourist ideology, for example: '*successful outcomes*', '*what works*' and '*varying condition*'. When looking at the other statements ranked highest by those exemplifying this viewpoint, one found '*developing functional communication*', '*reducing inappropriate and disruptive behaviours*', and '*promoting independence*'. This factor was found to be prevalent amongst non-autistic parents of autistic children. The most exemplifying individual Q-sort for this factor was that of participant P20, who in saying why they rated the statement regarding *developing functional communication'* as of utmost importance said:

> *'Because otherwise he is trapped in a world where he cannot communicate his hopes and fears, particularly when I am dead and cannot look out for him.'* (Participant P20)

To *'functionally communicate'* is seen as a primary aim for this participant, a mother to an autistic child, who indicated that she used the ABA-based practices. Within this narrative is that of the autistic child *'being trapped in a world'*. Yet, this is set against the prospect of an autistic child unable to communicate and thus advocate for their needs being met. This becomes a palpable fear for parents regarding *'when I am dead and cannot look out for him'*. Similarly, when asked why participant P20 also rated *'reducing inappropriate and disruptive behaviour'* of utmost importance, s/he talked about aggressive behaviour and self-harming, and the prospect of this leading to residential care.

Those exemplifying a factor 1 viewpoint rated statements related to pupil-led activities and critical pedagogy low, and by comparison to other factors rated liberal humanist ideology and the priority of basing education on 'evidence-based practice' relatively highly. Education from this viewpoint is framed within a seemingly normative perspective:

> *'...of the skills required in order to navigate the world as an adult.'* (Participant P20)

Not doing so was seen as a form of neglect or discrimination, reducing expectations and preventing the development of *'functional skills'*, and leaving autistic people to be 'in their own world' or left with their 'obsessions'. Such a narrative seemingly utilises a normative and/or medical/deficit model of autism being applied to what autism is. As an example, the narrative constructions of those exemplifying a factor 1 viewpoint utilised normative expectations as justifications with phrases used by participants such as *'no child in education...'* and *'ultimately children need...'*.

Factor 1 indicated a point of view that would appear against radical/critical pedagogy, whilst being in favour of a normative functionalist or behavioural approach that addresses perceived challenges located primarily in the autistic learner. The very low score attained by the statement: *'helping people on the autism spectrum become indistinguishable from their peers'* by those exemplifying a factor 1 viewpoint would indicate that full 'normalisation' is not the intent of this point of view however. Whilst being 'indistinguishable' is not a goal for those exemplifying factor 1, looking to equip autistic children with 'skills' to navigate a normative social environment is highly prioritised. This data would suggest that factor 1 displays a viewpoint akin to the theory of Positive Behaviour Support (PBS) (Hastings, 2013) and is the viewpoint with the most influence over parental accounts within the sample.

The statements that distinguish factor 1 from all the other extracted factors to a statistically significant level were the need for educational priorities to be informed by evidence-based practice, and most significantly, those exemplifying factor 1 rated: '*celebrating learners and not trying to 'normalise' them*' in the negative.

Although like factor 1, a tailored curriculum was rated highly, those exemplifying a factor 2 viewpoint indicated a perspective in favour of radical and progressive principles and interactionist practice, rating highly statements such as: '*celebrating learners and not trying to 'normalise' them*', '*radical change in society*', '*empowering students to be active and critical in their learning*', and '*utilising the interests of learners*'. Factor 2 can be seen to thus be anti-normative in its approach:

'*Because being normal isn't being happy.*' (Participant P19)

'*Difference should be accommodated, accepted and celebrated.*' (Participant P47)

The accounts of those exemplifying the factor 2 perspective indicated an anti-normalisation stance indicative of a 'neurodiversity paradigm' and social model of disability (Walker, 2014). Seeking normalcy in these accounts is seen as a damaging pursuit or abhorrent, with effort needed to reduce social marginalisation. The approach highlighted by factor 2 is also clearly against a normative functionalist or behaviourist theory and practice, with the following statements rated negatively: '*reducing inappropriate and disruptive behaviours*', '*addressing the core deficits of learners*', '*every moment being seen as an opportunity for reinforcing learning*'. The factor 2 perspective largely rejected Liberal Humanist views (as opposed to factor 1), stating progressive or radical viewpoints to support their reasoning. Of the eleven participants who exemplified factor 2, eight of them were autistic and five of these participants had multiple roles regarding their engagement with the field of autism. Of the three participants exemplifying this factor, who were not identifying themselves as being on the autism spectrum, one was a mother of a child in a mainstream school setting, and two were practitioners.

Both the distinguishing statements for factor 2 indicated areas of radical / progressive ideology. Firstly, the statement: *'pupils decide how to spend their time'*, was marked somewhat neutrally by those exemplifying factor 2, yet this was significantly different to the other factors which all marked the statement very negatively. Similarly, but to a greater level of statistical significance were responses to the statement: *'equality of status between staff and pupils'* which was rated in the positive by those exemplifying factor 2 and in the negative by all the other factors.

Those exemplifying factors 3-8 along with participants not exemplifying any of the factors were seen in the data to occupy various *'middle-ground'* positions in-between the positions being stated by factors 1 and 2, with some being influenced by differing aspects of each, often being less radical in orientation than either positions.

Figure 1 shows a scatter-plot distribution for all 60 individual Q-sorts for those who participated in the study plotted against their correlation to factors 1 (x-axis) and 2 (y-axis):

Figure 1: Individual Q-sort correlation with factors 1 and 2

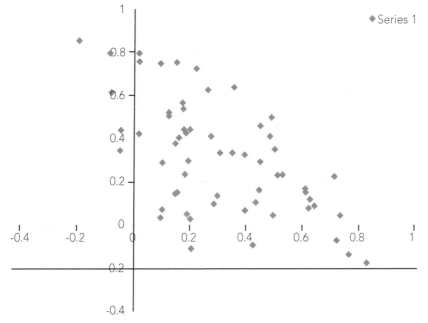

X = Factor 1 correlation score, Y = Factor 2 correlation score.

Note: Exemplifying Q-sorts for each factor would usually score above 0.6.

Figure 1 indicates the clumping of Q-sorts that rise above a score of 0.6 for either factor, and that the more one is influenced by one factor the less one is likely to be influenced by the other. There are some participants scoring somewhat highly in both and some scoring low in both factors, however. In relation to those Q-sorts that scored a correlation below 0.6 in either factor's 1 or 2, they either exemplified other factors (factors 3 to 8) or none at all. One could say that all fall on a spectrum between factors 1 and 2, but also show significant dissimilarities from one another, otherwise there would not have been 8 factors extracted from the data, however small the effect some of these factors were having on the overall sample distribution.

Figure 2: Spectrum of educational views by participant grouping

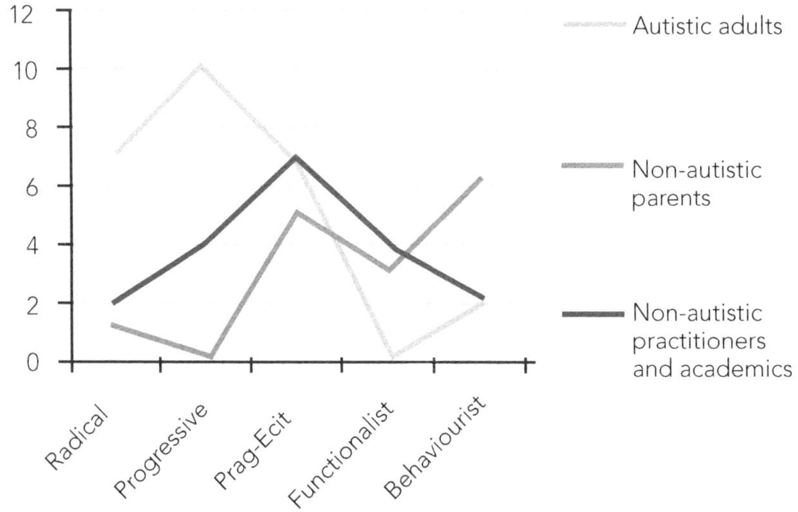

The chart in Figure 2 gives a simple indication of the different views of stakeholders grouped by their respective correlations to factors 1 and 2 (categorised as ranging from radical through to progressive, pragmatic, eclectic, functionalist, and behaviourist). The chart shows that there is a skewing of distributions of views of autistic and non-autistic parents from the middle-ground, whilst the practitioners and academics who participated in the study showed an even distribution across the educational ideology spectrum.

Discussion

When looking at the distribution of data between participant groupings evident in the findings of this study, one can see a three-way split with an autistic adult view highlighting a critical pedagogical ideology, non-autistic parents prioritising a more liberal humanist ideology and practice based on a Positive Behavioural Support (PBS) style of approach, and practitioners and academics often taking up a pragmatic or potentially eclectic middle ground position between the two. For non-autistic practitioners and academics there did not appear to be a consensus behind a coherent / dominant set of beliefs and practices that they adhered to as a group, but an array of positions taken up between those espousing a factor 1 or 2 viewpoint. It should be remembered too, that these were tendencies within the data and there was much diversity of views within each participant / stakeholder grouping, and that the findings from this sample may not be at all generalisable to a wider population of people. Yet, what is behind this three-way split in disposition and related educational priorities? Why does splitting the data into these three groupings produce such differing results?

Such a difference of view presents a number of common areas of concern within the context of education as problematic. For example, is the avoidance of demands a rational rebellion against a prejudicial and unfriendly social environment, or a pathological deficit in need of remedial strategies? Does promoting independence mean promoting self-advocacy and autonomy or doing things for oneself? Should more educational activities be led by pupil interests or fewer? Are intense autistic interests to be viewed as an autistic learning style to be nurtured and utilised as intrinsic motivation within classroom activities, or seen as something to be used as reinforcement for appropriate behaviour or as potentially dangerous 'obsessions'?

A fundamental tension between views was evident in the diversity of responses regarding the notion of 'evidence-based practice'. Interestingly, it was the non-autistic parents in favour of factor 1 who favoured this narrative significantly more than the other factors (and hence practitioners, academics and autistic adults). Perhaps there was a stronger narrative need for parents to be seen to base their decisions on received wisdom and a perceived state of evidence than it was for practitioners and academics working in the field of autism? It may be the case that the lower priority given to this narrative by practitioners, academics and autistic adults would be how the term has been debased by its over-usage, or that there are too many examples of when it is claimed without much to support it (in their view), or its connotations with normative and medical model perspectives?

Normalisation to the point of being indistinguishable from one's peers was rejected across the board by virtually all participants in the study. Thus an initial claim that can be made from this data sample is that there was a consensus over the rejection of the educational priorities as set out by Lovaas (1987). Many of the accounts linked whether someone should take a more medical or social model approach to an autistic person and their resultant educational priorities to where someone was deemed to be 'on the spectrum'. Those seen to be more severely affected were seen to be more impaired and treated more frequently in a normative fashion, whilst those deemed less so, seen as more in need of understanding and respect on their own terms. One could interpret the data as showing a split in views between autistic adults able to articulate their concerns and take part in such a study, and parents of less verbal 'low-functioning' children. However, this would be to miss the point that many of the autistic adults who participated were also parents of autistic children with more 'complex' or 'severe' needs (if viewed from a more functionalist perspective), yet took up a radical viewpoint akin to factor 2. Whilst some exemplifying a factor 1 viewpoint espoused a need for discipline and hierarchy in the classroom and those exemplifying a factor 2 viewpoint a more pupil-led approach, there was a general consensus that educational activities should be mutual and neither too learner or teacher-led.

Given the data provided from this sample of merely 60 participants, it is clear that a genuine consensus between differing stakeholders and dispositional outlooks regarding educational priorities for autistic children is highly unlikely. Only one statement out of forty-two gained general consensus to a statistically significant level: *'good communications between staff, pupils and parents'* and this was a consensus of mild agreement. There was however, a general favouring amongst the sixty participants toward an approach that considered the environment around the autistic learner and how enabling/disabling this can be. These areas were particularly noted by autistic participants and a number of practitioners in the sample. Such areas were also strongly highlighted by the autistic children and young people who participated in the consultation exercises for the Autism Education Trust's School Standards (Milton & Giannadou, 2012). There was also a general favouring of the category of 'building relationships' in general. A starting point that stakeholder's of all inclinations may agree on, would be the need to build better understanding and communications between all involved in the field of autism. It would appear that those at opposite ends of the ideological / dispositional spectrum are literally 'talking a different language'. This analysis highlights concerns that can be mapped against the educational priority areas that were devised by the Autism Education Trust (Guldberg *et al*, 2012) in building their training and support materials for educational practitioners, these being: Understanding the Individual Child, Enabling Environments, Curriculum and Learning, and Building Relationships.

Conclusion

When examining the field of autism, one can see that a number of communities of practice (Wenger, 1998) have evolved in relative isolation to one another. From autistic self-advocacy groups, through communities of practice that have developed through a particular academic discipline or paradigm, to parent support groups and forums, and professional conferences, one can see that many communities of practice exist. Each of these communities produces their own language, their own culture, and their own sets of resources and materials. The extent that there have been shared practices between these communities, however, has been traditionally at their respective fringes. Such a separation of related communities is a significant issue within the field of autism, and can be said to be largely responsible (combined with potential embodied differences of perception) for the 'three-way dispositional problem' found in the data of this study. One of the downsides of communities of practice, is that they develop in ways in which their shared competencies, experiences and practices, distinguish them from other groups, both providing a sense of identity and pride for their members, but also potentially fermenting a disparaging view regarding 'outsiders', especially if holding opposing views and performing practices that would seem somehow abhorrent to those within one's own group. Such disparities can easily lead to apathy, dyspathy (Cameron, 2012), and antipathy and/or stigma toward others. Therefore, to limit the effects of the 'silo mentality' (Arnold, 2010), the barriers separating these communities need to be reduced and collaborative communities of practice need to be established in order that stakeholders do not feel alienated and disenfranchised. This is easier said than done, however, when autistic activists have felt excluded from debates.

For inclusive practice to flourish, autistic people (along with stakeholders with non-autistic dispositions) need to feel a sense of belonging within collaborative communities of practice. It is hoped here that the example set by the efforts made by the Participatory Autism Research Collective (PARC) (www.PARCautism.co.uk), the AET (Guldberg *et al*, 2012; Jones et al, 2012; Wittemeyer *et al*, 2012), the Ask autism project (NAS, 2015), the Theorising Autism Project (Greenstein, 2014), the Autonomy journal (www.larry-arnold.net/Autonomy/index.php), Autscape (www.autscape.org), and other such endeavours can act as a signpost for all seeking to build bridges across dispositional divides.

References

ABA4all (2014) *Not Another Waffly Piece of 'Guidance'* [online]. https://www.facebook.com/ABAforallchildren/posts/686140071463809 (accessed August 2015).

Arnold L (2010) *The Medium is the Message* [online]. https://www.ucl.ac.uk/cpjh/Arnold (accessed February 2015).

Brown S (1978) The importance of factors in Q methodology: statistical and theoretical considerations. *Operant Subjectivity* **1** (4) 117–124.

Brown S (1980) *Political subjectivity: Applications of Q methodology in political science*. New Haven: Yale University Press.

Cameron L (2012) *Dyspathy: The dynamic complement of empathy*. Milton Keynes: Open University.

Cumine V, Leach J & Stevenson G (1998) *Asperger Syndrome: A practical guide for teachers*. London: David Fulton.

Greenstein A (2014) Theorising autism project – engaging autistic people in the research process. Review of a seminar day at the Institute of Education. *Autonomy, the Critical Journal of Interdisciplinary Autism Studies* **1** (3).

Guldberg K, Bradley R, Cooper R, Jones G, Mackness J, Makriyannis E, Milton D, Waltz M & Wittemeyer K (2012) *The Autism Education Trust Training Hubs Materials*. Autism Education Trust.

Hagland C & Webb Z (2009) *Working with Adults with Asperger Syndrome: A practical toolkit*. London: Jessica Kingsley.

Hanbury M (2005) *Educating Pupils with Autistic Spectrum Disorders: A practical guide*. London: Sage.

Hastings R (2013) *Behavioural method is not an attempt to 'cure' autism* [online]. Available at: https://theconversation.com/behavioural-method-is-not-an-attempt-to-cure-autism-19782 (accessed September 2017).

Hewitt S (2005) *Specialist Support Approaches to Autism Spectrum Disorder Students in Mainstream Settings*. London: Jessica Kingsley.

Humphrey N & Lewis S (2008) Make me normal: the views and experiences of pupils on the autism spectrum in mainstream secondary schools. *Autism* **12** (1) 23–46.

Jones G (2002) *Educational Provision for Children with Autism and Asperger Syndrome*. Abingdon: David Fulton.

Jones G, English A, Guldberg K, Jordan R, Richardson P & Waltz M (2008) *Educational Provision for Children and Young People on the Autism Spectrum Living in England: A review of current practice, issues and challenges*. London: Autism Education Trust.

Jones G, Baker L, English A & Lyn-Cook L (2012) *AET national autism standards for schools and educational settings*. London: Autism Education Trust.

Jordan RR (2009) Medicalisation of autism spectrum disorders: implications for services? *Journal of Hospital Medicine* **70** (3) 128–9.

Lawson W (2010) *The Passionate Mind: How people with autism learn*. London: Jessica Kingsley.

Lilley R (2015) Trading places: 'autism inclusion disorder' and school change. *Journal of Inclusive Education* **19** (4) 379–396.

Lovaas O (1987) Behavioural treatment and normal educational and intellectual functioning in young autistic children, *Journal of Consulting and Clinical Psychology,* **55** 3–9.

Maurice C (1993) *Let Me Hear Your Voice: A family's triumph over autism.* London: Robert Hale.

Milton D & Giannadou K (2012) *Views of Children and Young People with Autism On: What makes a good school for pupils with autism* [online]. London: Autism Education Trust. Available at: www.aettraininghubs.org.uk/wp-content/uploads/2012/05/2.3-33.2-Pupils-views-on-school.pdf (accessed September 2017).

National Autistic Society (NAS) (2015) *Ask Autism* [online]. Available at: www.autism.org.uk/our-services/training-and-consultancy/ask-autism.aspx (accessed August 2015).

Parsons S, Guldberg K, Macleod A, Jones G, Prunty A & Balfe T (2009) *International Review of Evidence of Best Practice Provision in the Education of Persons with Autistic Spectrum Disorders.* Trim: National Council for Special Education.

Sainsbury C (2000) *Martian in the Playground: Understanding the schoolchild with Asperger's syndrome.* Bristol: Lucky Duck.

Scrimshaw P (1983) *Educational Ideologies.* Milton Keynes: Open University.

Senior B & Viveash M (1998) *Health and Illness.* Basingstoke: Palsgrave.

Stephenson W (1935) Correlating persons instead of tests. *Character and Personality,* **4** 17–24.

Stephenson W (1953) *The Study of Behavior: Q-technique and its methodology.* Chicago: University of Chicago Press.

Thomas D & Baas L (1992) The issue of generalisation in Q methodology: 'reliable schematics' revisited. *Operant Subjectivity* **16** (1) 18–36.

Van Exel J & de Graaf G (2005) *Q Methodology: A sneak preview* [online]. See: www.jobvanexel.nl (accessed January 2013).

Walker N (2014) *Neurodiversity: Some basic terms & definitions* [online]. Available: http://neurocosmopolitanism.com/neurodiversity-some-basic-terms-definitions/ (accessed September 2017).

Waltz M (2013) *Autism: A social and medical history.* London: Palgrave Macmillan.

Watts S & Stenner P (2012) Doing Q Methodological Research: Theory, method and interpretation. London: Sage.

Wenger E (1998) *Communities of Practice: Learning, meaning, and identity.* Cambridge: Cambridge University Press.

Wittemeyer K, English A, Jones G, Lyn-Cook L & Milton D (2012) *The Autism Education Trust Professional Competency Framework.* Autism Education Trust.

Worth S (2005) *Autistic Spectrum Disorders (SEN Series).* London: Continuum.

Zurcher A (2012) *Tackling That Troublesome Issue of ABA and Ethics* [online]. Available at: http://emmashopebook.com/2012/10/10/tackling-that-troublesome-issue-of-aba-and-ethics/ (accessed September 2017).

BV - #0097 - 211123 - C0 - 210/148/12 - PB - 9781911028765 - Gloss Lamination